Geographic Data Imperfection 1

Geographic Data Imperfection 1

From Theory to Applications

Edited by

Mireille Batton-Hubert
Eric Desjardin
François Pinet

WILEY

First published 2019 in Great Britain and the United States by ISTE Ltd and John Wiley & Sons, Inc.

ISTE Ltd
27-37 St George's Road
London SW19 4EU
UK

www.iste.co.uk

John Wiley & Sons, Inc.
111 River Street
Hoboken, NJ 07030
USA

www.wiley.com

Library of Congress Control Number: 2019938868

British Library Cataloguing-in-Publication Data
A CIP record for this book is available from the British Library
ISBN 978-1-78630-297-7

MIX
Paper from
responsible sources
FSC® C013604

Contents

Chapter 8. Reasoning in Modal Logic for Uncertain Data . . .   133
Élisabeth GAVIGNET and Nadine CULLOT

Chapter 9. Reviewing the Qualifiers of Imperfection in Geographic Information   151
Giovanni FUSCO and Andrea TETTAMANZI

Chapter 10. The Features of Decision Aid and Analysis Processes in Geography: How to Grasp Complexity, Uncertainty, and Risks?.   175
Myriam MERAD

Preface

Geomatics is a scientific field that in the last 30 years has become closely intwined with our everyday life, to such an extent that we often forget all its underlying challenges. Who does not have a navigation application on his or her mobile phone? Who does not manipulate geolocated data? In the coming decades, the volumes of georeferenced data generated should increase dramatically.

This book focuses on the notion of imperfection in geographic data, which is a significant topic in geomatics. In fact, it is essential to define and represent the imperfection that may affect geographic data. Uncertainty constitutes the basis of the study of the so-called modern probability, a field that became very active in the 18th century (thanks to the works carried out by P. de Fermat, B. Pascal, Th. Bayes, P. S. Laplace, and several others) and was complemented by concepts developed in the 19th century and, more particularly, later in the 20th century. The notion of imperfection supplements this concept; the single representation of the stochastic (random) nature of a fact is limited when the aim is to represent the precision of a fact and/or the lack of knowledge about data. These theories, which deal with these two aspects, were complemented in particular by the Dempster–Shafer theory.

A better awareness of this imperfection, which is linked specifically to geographic data, especially during the formalization, storage, and manipulation of this characteristic, improves their analyses and any decision-analysis process. Even if it is important (and even critical) to manage imperfection, it must be acknowledged that integrating it into data-processing procedures may be challenging. To take up this challenge, this book intends to bridge the gap between the need and its implementation. It simultaneously explores theoretical aspects, in order to illustrate more clearly phenomena and representations, and practical/pragmatic aspects by presenting concrete examples and applied tools.

This book was written in the context of an initiative of the *Groupement de Recherche du CNRS sur les Méthodes et Applications pour la Géomatique et l'Information Spatiale* (*GDR MAGIS*) (Associated Research of the CNRS on the Methods and Uses of Geomatics and Spatial Information). This initiative, which targeted the uncertainty of spatial data, gave rise to a specific work group which took part in writing this book. Thus, this book is the common product of an analysis of this topic. It is our hope that it will manage to meet the readers' expectations.

We would like to express our sincere thanks to the authors of the various chapters and, more generally, to all the individuals who took part in the work groups of the GDR MAGIS over time. We extend our thanks to them for their fruitful ideas, which have made it possible to elaborate further on the ideas expressed in this book. We would like to thank the GDR MAGIS of the CNRS as well as its various directors for their support and their trust in this project.

We hope that readers will enjoy this book and that it will shed some light on the methods that make it possible to better understand and process geographic imperfections.

The editors of this book and the organizers of the initiative *Incertitude épistémique – des données aux modèles en géomatique* (*Epistemic Uncertainty – from Data to Models in Geomatics*) of the GDR MAGIS of the CNRS:

Mireille BATTON-HUBERT
Eric DESJARDIN
François PINET
May 2019

Part 1

Bases and Concepts

Imperfection and Geographic Information

"We should learn to navigate on a sea of uncertainties,
sailing in and around islands of certainty"

Edgar Morin, *Seven Complex Lessons in Education for the Future* (*2000*)

"Uncertainty is not in things but in our head: uncertainty
is a lack of knowledge"

Jacques Bernoulli, *Ars Conjectandi* (*1713*)

1.1. Context

Today, geographic information is everywhere. With the constant development of new information and communication technologies, we are witnessing a significant increase in the number of sources of georeferenced data. Data are acquired by IT (information technology) means, such as connected objects, computers, mobile equipment, and through remote sensing, and are then processed in Geographic Information Systems (GISs). The increasing systematization of the automated acquisition of geographic data is paving the way for ever more numerous and complex applications.

In several fields, the terms "data" and "information" are quite often considered to be interchangeable. Yet, many distinguish between the concept

Chapter written by François PINET, Mireille BATTON-HUBERT and Eric DESJARDIN.

of information and that of data [COO 17]. A piece of data corresponds to a value. It may be seen as the assignment of values to properties, for example, City = "Paris". Sometimes, the types of data are complex, as is the case for multimedia data. When data are processed, organized together, and structured in a precise context, we refer to it as information. In IT, knowledge often corresponds to rules and models that rely on information [BEL 04]. A knowledge base will make it possible, among other things, to reason and make deductions [ABI 00, NIL 90].

Information and data may be geographic or spatial [BEA 19]. "Geographic" is the adjective used when we refer to the Earth. In the field on which this book focuses, the term "spatial" usually refers to a localization (coordinates, topology, etc.) in some type of space (whether geographic or not). A spatial or geographic object has a geometry (a dimension, a shape, some coordinates) that may be more or less known or established. Different properties may be assigned to the object depending on its meaning. The field that studies the methods and technologies linked to geographic information (from its acquisition to its dissemination) is called "geomatics". The geomatic paradigm was born in Canada [BÉD 07].

Objects are often affected by imperfections. In the literature, various terms are used to refer to these imperfections, so it is difficult to put forward only one type of terminology. Depending on the points of view, the same term may be defined in a different manner.

The imperfection of information and geographic data is often neglected so, occasionally, there are risks involved when using them [BÉD 86, EDO 15]. For example, these risks are significant when data are used to help decision-making. Imperfection often derives from a restriction that hinders the correct identification of an object and/or the accurate measurement of its properties [BÉD 86]. In most cases, a representation said to be certain is used even if the object has not been completely defined. There will be a difference between the object and its representation. Finding out this difference is indeed a difficult and intricate task. Conveying this difference implies an "actual world" independent of the observer. This is often difficult and complex [BÉD 86] as the objects of the actual world are in general perceived and known through observations. According to [FIS 99], the main problem concerns the way in which a data collector and a data user understand the natures of uncertainties, which may be of different kinds.

As this book demonstrates, it is possible to avoid overlooking data imperfection. There are solutions that allow us to manipulate imperfect geographic data effectively. Over time, various specific techniques and methods have been put forward to define, represent, and deal with the imperfection of a geographic object. Each of them may be used in relation to the level of quality expected and the application targeted. As [EDO 15] and [BÉD 86] recall, using imperfect data may indeed be acceptable for some uses but not for others. This book aims to present some of the techniques and methods used to manage the imperfection of geographic data.

In order to give a (very general) trend to the theme of uncertainty of spatial data in the scientific domain, in Table 1.1 and in Figure 1.1, we present the search results in Scopus, a bibliographical and scientific database. A 25-year interval (1994–2018) is considered. Column A indicates the number of scientific publications whose keywords include the terms "spatial data" and "uncertainty". Column B shows the number of publications that include "spatial data" in their keywords. Column C shows the ratio A/B over these 25 years, which corresponds to 2.25%. The chosen terms, i.e. "spatial data" and "uncertainty", are quite emblematic of the topic we are focused on. Yet, the Scopus searches could certainly be refined, especially through a test with various keywords of concepts related to data and spatialized information as well as imprecision.

In this chapter, we will introduce the different parts of this book while also revealing which issues they tackle. We have chosen to structure this book into three different sections: an introduction of the foundations and main concepts, a part on the modes of representation, and then a description of reasoning systems and processes.

1.2. Concepts, representation, reasoning system, and data processing

1.2.1. *Foundations and concepts*

The first part describes the foundations and main concepts related to the imperfection of geographic data. The issue is to shed light on and provide a summary of terminologies, the origins of imperfections, as well as the concepts of quality, integrity, and confidence.

The main goal of this chapter is to clarify the terminology and the definitions assigned to various concepts that revolve around the imperfection and uncertainty of geographic information. These terms have been used in different ways over the years. This chapter will underline some definitions that can be found in the field. The analysis put forward does not lead to a new terminology. Rather, it brings into relief the diversity of uses while also highlighting the main differences and similarities between the concepts and the terminologies.

Chapter 2 introduces the principal sources of imperfections. It attempts to answer the following question: "where do the imperfections of geographic data originate?". Naturally, there is more than one answer to this question. There are different causes behind these imperfections. One of the aims of this chapter is to show and illustrate imperfection at various points during the life cycle of geographic information.

Chapter 3 provides a basic explanation of the quality and integrity of data. On several occasions, it recalls standard quality criteria as well as the way in which they are assessed. This chapter establishes the notions of data integrity and confidence, and it concretely illustrates the various problems related to these concepts through examples drawn from the field of maritime navigation.

1.2.2. *Representations of imperfection*

Part 2 tackles the main representations of imperfection and their applications for geographic information.

Chapter 5 describes various modeling formalisms, especially fuzzy sets and the means of representing confidence and certainty (probability, possibility, necessity, etc.). It also presents the operations used to manipulate these concepts and reveals how spatial entities like broad boundary objects and fuzzy objects can be modeled.

Chapter 6 focuses on the representation of classes of objects. When several objects share the same properties and are of the same type, they can be grouped into classes. Elements of the same class share the same characteristics. Thus, establishing classes denotes identifying the points in common among the various entities. Defining classes is very important when a dataset must be described. This chapter reveals how it is possible to describe data imperfection when drawing class diagrams.

1.2.3. *Reasoning systems and data processing*

Part 3 introduces a few data processing and reasoning systems that involve spatial objects. Imperfection is considered in relation to our knowledge about the objects.

Chapter 7 concerns the spatial relations among objects. It reveals how it is possible to reason specifically about these relations and then move on to modeling these relations on imperfect objects such as broad boundary objects in space.

Chapter 8 deals with a type of knowledge that is founded on rules and deduction. This chapter provides rational approaches that employ a type of modeling based on the rules in first-order logic and then in modal logic. Modal logic can describe uncertainties. This chapter includes an example involving geographic data so that this approach can be understood.

Chapter 9 deals with the case involving the gradual acquisition of information and the repeated revision of the state of knowledge. This necessity is all the more significant as geographic data may be acquired in various ways over time and their sources may be heterogeneous depending on the case. This chapter focuses on the belief revision of imperfect information, especially Bayesian revisions and alternatives in non-probabilistic formalisms.

Chapter 10 considers on an operational level the awareness in decision-support processes of uncertainties, representations, and perceptions of the territory. Choosing a suitable approach is a difficult issue: the potential variety of the number of formalisms employed to deal with these aspects in relation to the types of management is an issue tackled in this chapter. Chapter 10 highlights that the decision-support process may be of a specific kind when it is managed by an analyst/geographer and when it addresses the question of multi-criteria approaches and risk analyses.

1.3. Some conclusive remarks

This book aims to present an analysis of the imperfection of spatial information and its origins as well as to group together various descriptions of methods that can be useful for representing, reasoning about, and processing this information. In order to make its content more intuitive, this work provides various illustrations chapter after chapter in various applications.

Years	A: keywords "spatial data" "uncertainty"	B: keyword "spatial data"	A/B
1994	2	75	2.67%
1995	0	62	0.00%
1996	1	75	1.33%
1997	3	80	3.75%
1998	2	73	2.74%
1999	1	68	1.47%
2000	8	168	4.76%
2001	3	131	2.29%
2002	2	161	1.24%
2003	7	214	3.27%
2004	6	286	2.10%
2005	15	427	3.51%
2006	13	456	2.85%
2007	19	504	3.77%
2008	22	770	2.86%
2009	14	1084	1.29%
2010	29	1106	2.62%
2011	25	1001	2.50%
2012	17	923	1.84%
2013	17	835	2.04%
2014	12	756	1.59%
2015	14	759	1.84%
2016	20	825	2.42%
2017	17	812	2.09%
2018	10	775	1.29%
	279	12426	2.25%

Table 1.1. *Evolution of the appearance of the terms "spatial data" and "uncertainty" from 1994 to 2018 in the keywords of publications (Scopus – January 30, 2019)*

Naturally, this work does not treat the topic exhaustively, but it allows us to take into consideration various points related to managing imperfection in geographic information. According to us, it is advisable to pay more attention to the imperfection of spatial data, in order to improve and increase the reliability of the future use of geographic information. The use of geographic data should tend to speed up so it is quite likely that being aware of these issues will become more and more important in quite a few areas of application.

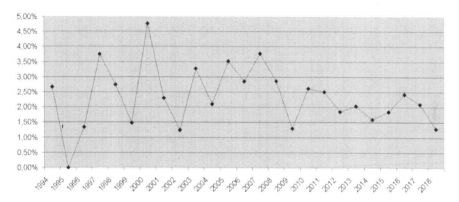

Figure 1.1. *A chart of the ratio A/B of Table 1.1*

1.4. References

[ABI 00] ABITEBOUL S., HULL R., VIANU V., *Fondements des bases de données*, Vuibert, Paris, 2000.

[BEA 19] BEAL V., Spatial Data, available at: https://www.webopedia.com/ TERM/S/spatial_data.html, 2019.

[BÉD 07] BÉDARD Y., "Geomatics. 26 years of history already!", *Geomatica*, vol. 61, no. 3, pp. 269–272, 2007.

[BÉD 86] BÉDARD Y., "A study of data using a communication based conceptual framework of land information systems", (updated version), *The Canadian Surveyor*, vol. 40, no. 4, pp. 449–460, 1986.

[BEL 04] BELLINGER G., CASTRO D., MILLS A., *Data, Information, Knowledge, and Wisdom*, available at: http://www.systems-thinking.org/dikw/dikw.htm, 2004.

[COO 17] COOPER P., "Data, information, knowledge and wisdom", *Anaesthesia & Intensive Care Medicine*, vol. 18, no. 1, pp. 55–56, 2017.

[EDO 15] EDOH-ALOVE D.E.A., Handling spatial vagueness issues in SOLAP datacubes by introducing a risk-aware approach in their design, PhD thesis, Université Blaise Pascal – Clermont-Ferrand II, Université Laval Québec, available at: https://tel.archives-ouvertes.fr/tel-01875720, 2015.

[FIS 99] FISHER P.F., "Models of uncertainty in spatial data", in LONGLEY P., GOODCHILD M., MAGUIRE D. *et al.* (eds), *Geographical Information Systems: Principles, Techniques, Management and Applications*, vol. 1, John Wiley & Sons, New York, 1999.

[NIL 90] NILSSON U., MATUSZYNSKI J., *Logic, Programming and Prolog*, Wiley, Chichester, 1990.

Imperfection of Geographic Information: Concepts and Terminologies

2.1. Introduction

Geographic information results from a process, which is often complex, that implies collecting information about the so-called "real" world, abstracting and simplifying it so that it can be represented in an environment which is in general digital. A process of this kind cannot, and should not, capture the world in all its complexity. Some of these induced/generated imperfections are accidental (like errors created during the collection of data), whereas others may have been introduced on purpose (cartographic generalization) to provide a simplified view of the world that corresponds to the needs of a specific community of users. The sources and nature of these imperfections have been relatively well-known, described, and assessed/ qualified/measured for a long time in cartography. This body of knowledge was integrated in the 1980s in Geographic Information Sciences (GISciences) and geomatics, as well as in various other fields (see, e.g. [BÉD 86, CHR 83, GOO 83, ROB 85] for discussions of these questions). Often identified as "errors" in early works [CHR 91, FIS 87, GOO 89], these imperfections were later described using a wider range of terms, which led them later on to fall under the two broad concepts of spatial uncertainty and data quality. There are several words employed to describe the differences between the world and its representation, and, depending on their nature or source, they are often associated with terms like accuracy, ambiguity, completeness, consistency, error, ignorance, imperfection, precision, quality, random nature, uncertainty, and vague/fuzzy. Even if a consensus has been

Chapter written by Rodolphe Devillers, Eric Desjardin and Cyril De Runz.

reached on the reasons behind the source of these imperfections, there are strongly divergent opinions about the terms used to describe each of these types, the exact meaning of these terms, and the way in which they interfere/interact with one another. Various authors have defined and even organized these terms within ontologies [BÉD 86, DUC 01, FIS 99, SMI 89], thus expressing a point of view on their definitions and relationships, but without necessarily looking for an agreement within the community on the use of a common terminology. Such a lack of consensus about a common language has been criticized in the past and was considered to negatively affect some of the research carried out by the various communities interested in geographic information (see, e.g. [DEV 10]).

Fisher [FIS 03], for instance, has criticized the general lack of links between the fields that study spatial uncertainty and spatial data quality. This argument was developed later on by [COM 06]. Fisher uses the analogy of "ships passing in the night", where two ships (i.e. the fields of "uncertainty" and "data quality") may be quite close in space without necessarily seeing each another).

Here, we aim to shed some light on this topic, potentially helping these ships and perhaps others to see each other more clearly and understand what makes them similar or different.

This introductory chapter does not aim to provide a single authoritative terminology, or to create a new taxonomy, but, on the contrary, to acknowledge the various ways in which these terms are used in different fields. We will talk about these differences and similarities through the use of these terms by associating them with certain causes that are at the root of these imperfections and the way they are used.

Section 2.2 discusses some terms used to describe spatial uncertainty, data quality, and their interrelations. Section 2.3 presents several taxonomies of spatial uncertainty or related concepts. Ultimately, section 2.4 presents a theoretical/conceptual framework that discusses the nature of the uncertainty and data quality, as well as the elements that they share or in which they differ.

2.2. Semantics according to Humpty Dumpty[1]

Uncertainties are inherent to various descriptions of our environment. When we describe our world, its large size and complexity force us to merely observe some of its parts (e.g. by sampling). Our representations are also necessarily simplified (e.g. by summarizing the information through descriptive statistics, by carrying out map generalization processes, or by combining information in sub-divisions of space such as pixels). Descriptions of our world, whether written, oral, or graphical, like books, paintings, or speeches, provide a piece of information about our environment which is, on different levels, incomplete and inaccurate. [BÉD 86] described this process very accurately in a modeling exercise necessary for the mapping communication process.

In common language, some words or tenses (e.g. the conditional) can be employed to characterize the level of certainty assigned to information and sometimes even suggest acceptable probability levels (e.g. [TEI 88]). For instance, it could be said that the economic crisis "might" continue next year, that the weather "will quite likely" be good tomorrow, or that we are "near" the end. In common language, a large number of words can also be used to describe the nature of uncertainties or imperfections. For example, information may be vague or ambiguous, an image may be blurry, a forecast may be accurate, and so on. While several languages have a rich vocabulary that can be used to represent these aspects, the meaning of these terms may be vague or unknown to most individuals. The definitions of these terms as they are given in dictionaries may not be very helpful, as a definition is often established by employing other related terms, often giving the impression that many of these terms can be used as synonyms (Figure 2.1). Some studies have also shown that similar words that describe uncertainty do not necessarily mean the same thing for individuals who speak different languages [DOU 03].

While some of these words may have similar meanings, others have clearly distinct meanings; for example, "accuracy" is perceived to be more similar to "precision" than "incompleteness" or "incoherence".

---

1 See the reference in Figure 2.2.

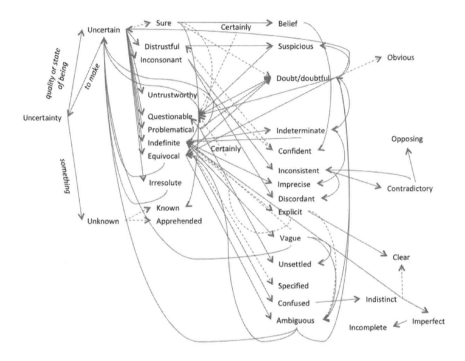

Figure 2.1. *Relations between different words found in the Webster English dictionary. Arrows link words (origin) whose definitions refer to other words (the arrowhead). Full arrows indicate positive relations, while the dotted arrows indicate negative relations (namely, when a word is defined by negating another word)*

While some words may mean the same thing for most individuals (e.g. the words "precise" and "accurate" are often regarded as synonymous in common parlance), other words may mean something different depending on the communities of individuals. Therefore, words can mean different things to individuals based on their experience or areas of expertise. People occasionally adopt intolerant behaviors toward those who use definitions that differ from theirs. This is not dissimilar from a comment made by Humpty Dumpty, a popular character from literature who appears in Lewis Carroll's *Through the Looking Glass, and What Alice Found There* [CAR 71]. Humpty Dumpty (Figure 2.2) is discussing semantics with Alice when he says: "When I use a word [...] it means just what I choose it to mean – neither more nor less". Similarly, several individuals or groups associate their own meanings to words, neither more nor less, sometimes adopting specific definitions for some terms that could have different meanings for other communities.

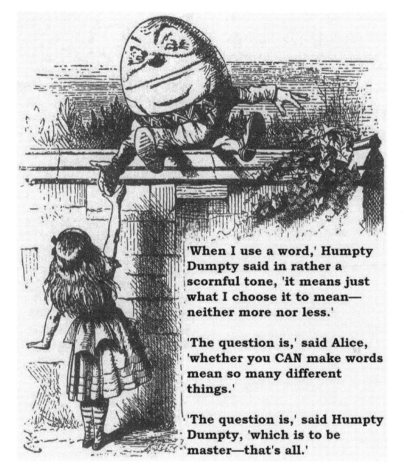

Figure 2.2. *An excerpt from* Through the Looking Glass, and What Alice Found There *[CAR 71]*

Diversity in the words used to describe uncertainty and imperfections in everyday speech can also be found in science. Subjects like statistics, economics, or medicine may assign different meanings to a same word or use two different words to refer to a same concept. This diversity can also be found in geomatics, a highly interdisciplinary field. For example, "uncertainty" and "error" are synonyms for some authors, whereas they mean different things for others. Authors can also assign different meanings to the same word. Table 2.1 illustrates this problem through examples of definitions of, or discussions about, "error" drawn from dictionaries and scientific articles. Smets [SME 97], for instance, puts forward a very broad definition of error by associating it with imperfect data. Several authors (e.g. [DEI 08, DUC 01], and the second and third Webster definitions in Table 2.1) provide a definition of error which resembles that of accuracy, whereas [NAV 06] puts it against accuracy. [SHI 09] associates error with uncertainty while acknowledging some differences, whereas [LON 05] refers to it in the more general context of "measurement".

Reference	Definition
Larousse	Something wrong, erroneous when compared to the truth, a standard or a rule (translated).
Wordnet	(Computer science) The occurrence of an incorrect result produced by a computer.
Merriam-Webster (1)	An act involving an unintentional deviation from truth or accuracy.
Merriam-Webster (2)	Something produced by mistake.
Merriam-Webster (3)	The difference between an observed or calculated value and a true value; specifically: variation in measurements, calculations, or observations of a quantity due to mistakes or to uncontrollable factors.
[DEI 08]	Difference between a measured or reported value and the true value, encompassing both precision and accuracy.
[DUC 01]	Error, or inaccuracy, concerns a lack of correlation of observation with reality.
[SHI 09]	In many cases, the term "error" is used as a synonym for uncertainty. However, it should be realized that the concept of error is, in fact, narrower.
[SME 97]	(Erroneous) beliefs, opinions, methods, etc. that are erroneous, incorrect, or only partly correct.
[BEA 89]	The term source error includes completeness and positional errors and attribute descriptions introduced during data collection. [...] Manipulations of the data subsequent to the collection, such as digital conversion, generalization, scale change, projections, and graphic representation can introduce additional errors. These errors will be referred to as process errors. [...] Use error will refer to the misinterpretation of maps or the misapplication of maps in tasks for which they are not appropriate.

[DER 11]	When an [...] object is well-defined but there is no evidence of the validity of the object, then the object is liable to error.
[CHR 91]	Quality is a neutral term, fitting for a national standard, but the tough issues of quality are best evoked by the loaded word "error". In common usage, an error is a bad thing, and many professions related to spatial data share this attitude.
[LON 05]	The established scientific notion of measurement *error* focuses on differences between observers or between measuring instruments.
Oxford Reference Online 1996 (quoted in [LEY 05])	Error, which includes inaccuracy in cases of systematic errors and imprecision in cases of random errors, is the difference between a computed, observed, or measured value or condition and the true, specified, or theoretically correct value or condition.
[NAV 06a]	The idea of errors is that data emerge from measurements and these measurements may be wrong. In contrast to accuracy in data quality here we do not assume a normal distribution for the measurements. We include systematic deviations and gross errors as well. The different aspects of error include accuracy, reliability, bias, precision, etc.

Table 2.1. *Different definitions of the word "error"*

2.3. Taxonomies of GI and its related uncertainty

Besides the differences between definitions, major differences can also be observed in the way in which people relate these terms by establishing taxonomies. While some use uncertainty as an overarching concept [FIS 99, ZHA 02], others prefer using imperfection [BOU 95, DUC 01, SME 97] or ignorance [SMI 89] (see Figure 2.3 for examples of taxonomies). If taxonomies' elements often use the same names, the respective meaning of each of them is not necessarily the same (e.g. Table 2.1). Furthermore, taxonomies, like several classifications, offer various ways of organizing a complex field. Even though taxonomies can be more or less useful for a community of users, they are not necessarily right or wrong; rather, they represent different ways of organizing a complex set of concepts.

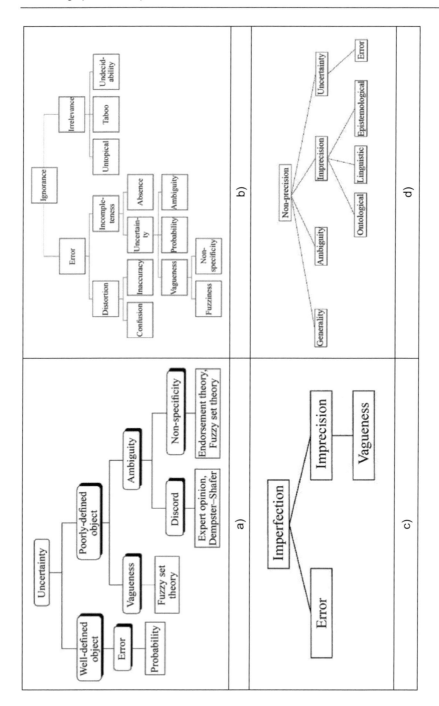

Figure 2.3. Examples of taxonomies: a) [FIS 06], b) [SMI 89], c) [DUC 01], and d) [NIS 89]

The taxonomies presented in Figure 2.3 consider this issue from several points of view. For example, [FIS 99] adopts an approach more orientated toward modeling/mapping and immediately distinguishes between the uncertainty related to well-defined objects (like a house or a road) and that related to ill-defined objects (like a mountain or a wetland). [SMI 89] focuses more generally on ignorance and differentiates between the state of ignorance (which he calls "error") and the act of ignoring, if knowledge is found to be irrelevant ("irrelevance"). According to Smithson, "uncertainty" is a type of "incompleteness", which is itself a type of "error". On the other hand, [NIS 89] and [ZHA 02] consider the question from the opposite perspective, regarding "error" as a type of "uncertainty".

When the definitions used by different authors are compared, it may become difficult to match these terminologies, given that the same terms can mean the same thing or sometimes be completely different.

Besides differences in the terms employed, their definitions, and their relations, there are also differences between authors in relation to the level of abstraction (data–information–knowledge) of the imperfection/uncertainty that they tackle. For example, while some discuss the incompleteness of data (for instance, how many objects are missing from a data set), others refer to the incompleteness of information or even knowledge. Similarly, authors do not necessarily associate each term with the same level.

2.4. A theoretical framework of the nature of uncertainty and quality

Despite the various and sometimes conflicting definitions used to describe the uncertainties/imperfections of geographic information, the literature generally agrees on the processes that cause uncertainty (e.g. [BÉD 86, COU 03, FIS 99, FRA 08, ROB 85]). Figure 2.4 sums up the theoretical framework within which uncertainty and quality issues take place, distinguishing between where data uncertainty takes shape and where data quality can be found, and identifying those cases in which specific types of problems occur.

Uncertainty issues emerge mostly from the process that generates representations (e.g. data) from the real world (see Figure 2.4). Even if this process is fairly complex, we can identify a few major steps that will affect the representations of the world. Humans create models that act as cognitive filters, structuring and simplifying the actual world with a specific goal in mind (e.g. the creation of maps for specific thematic areas like transportation). Models sample the world, focusing on specific features, simplifying its complexity, and describing objects by using specific properties as well as possible relationships among objects. This process gives rise to various differences between the real world and the model, leading to the lack of numerous details (namely, incomplete knowledge). Thus, when mapping a city, one can choose to map only buildings, roads, and rivers, deciding not to represent other features or levels of complexity. Similarly, models identify the specific properties of the objects that will be described, such as the area and the number of floors of buildings, but they may omit more specific features (e.g. the fact that the granite stairs leading to the main entrance of the building have seven steps of a given height and width). Besides, the modeling process forces the entities of the world to correspond to some constraints (e.g. semantic classifications or geometric forms), to simplify their characteristics, and to create even greater challenges for ill-defined objects (imprecision). Therefore, what was a complex group of trees in the real world could be represented as a polygon and described in a model by its estimated species composition. A modeling process such as this is linked to the creation of an ontology, and it has consequences on the uncertainty and quality of the resulting data [FRA 01, NAV 06b].

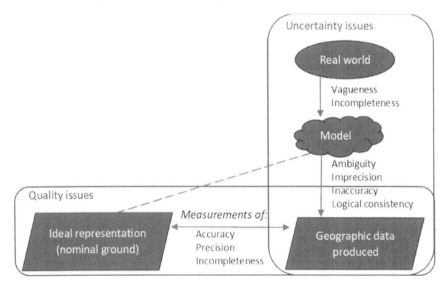

Figure 2.4. *A theoretical framework of uncertainty. For a color version of this figure, see www.iste.co.uk/batton/geographic1.zip*

The model is then translated into an actual, physical representation like a map or a database, widening the gap between the world and its representation. Information about the world may be acquired through different methods (e.g. land surveying, GPS, remote sensing) so that various levels of precision and accuracy are available. The description of the individual features of the actual world through the filter of the model may result in the fact that some characteristics are harder to classify than others (e.g. ambiguity). A representation may also represent a model inaccurately, leading to errors and problems related to logical consistency.

On the other hand, the quality of the data produced (sometimes called "internal quality" in this precise case) does not necessarily focus on the difference between the world and its representation. The goal is to compare a perfect representation, which represents the world through the lens of the model, with the representation that was actually produced (i.e. the data). In order to measure this internal quality, measurements should be taken to ensure that all the objects or descriptions to be mapped have indeed been mapped (e.g. completeness), etc. Another definition of quality, which is also common, is that of "external quality". This is a concept that refers to the suitability of a data set for specific uses (i.e. the concept of "fitness for use") – see [DEV 06]. In this context, the internal quality of a data set may be very high, but the data set may be unsuitable for some uses (e.g. a land tenure map may not be very useful in a geological analysis). Chapters 3 and 4 will discuss in more detail the concepts of internal and external quality.

Generally, we could say that quality is a bottom-up approach revolving mostly around data, whereas uncertainty is a top-down approach principally based on the levels of information and knowledge.

2.5. Conclusion

This chapter has provided a general introduction to the terminology used to describe the imperfections related to geographic information. This wealth of terminology, whose terms often mean different things in various fields (e.g. geomatics, geography, computer science, and mathematics), has been identified as a potential obstacle to the development of a cross-disciplinary approach adopted to deal with the imperfections of geographic information. At first, we highlighted the complexity inherent to this terminology, underscoring differences in the use of words not only between everyday speech and their meaning in the scientific field but also among various scientific communities. Then, we discussed several ways that were proposed for organizing these terms into taxonomies. These taxonomies aptly illustrate differences in the way in which this field may be conceptualized. Through these examples, we discussed the difficulty involved in putting forward a single terminology for all the fields associated with geographic/spatial information, and also questioned the relevance of such an approach. Ultimately, we looked at the more conceptual issues at the origin of these various imperfections, separating the problems related to uncertainty from those associated with data quality.

Some of the following chapters in this book will reconsider some notions presented in this chapter, making it possible to analyze more in depth some issues related to geographic data processing that can impact spatial uncertainty and data quality.

2.6. References

[BEA 89] BEARD K., "Use error: the neglected error component", *AUTO-CARTO 9*, Baltimore, MD, 1989.

[BÉD 86] BÉDARD Y., "A study of data using a communication based conceptual framework of land information systems", *The Canadian Surveyor*, no. 40, pp. 449–460, 1986.

[BOU 95] BOUCHON-MEUNIER B., *Logique floue et applications*, Addison-Wesley, Paris, 1995.

[CAR 71] CARROLL L., *Through the Looking Glass, and What Alice Found There*, Macmillan and Co., London, 1871.

[CHR 83] CHRISMAN N.R., "The role of quality information in the long-term functioning of a geographic information system", in WELLAR B. (ed), *AUTO-CARTO 6*, ASPRS, Ottawa, Canada, vol. 2, pp. 79–87, 1983.

[CHR 91] CHRISMAN N.R., "The error component in spatial data", in MAGUIRE D.J., GOODCHILD M.F., RHIND D.W. (eds), *Geographic Information Systems: Principles and Applications*, vol. IV, pp. 165–174, 1991.

[COM 06] COMBER A.J., FISHER P.F., HARVEY F. *et al.*, "Using metadata to link uncertainty and data quality assessments", in RIEDL A., KAINZ W., ELMES G. (eds), *12th International Symposium on Spatial Data Handling*, Berlin, Springer, pp. 279–292, 2006.

[COU 03] COUCLELIS H., "The certainty of uncertainty: GIS and the limits of geographic knowledge", *Transactions in GIS*, vol. 7, no. 2, pp. 165–175, 2003.

[DEI 08] DEITRICK S., EDSALL R., "Making uncertainty usable: approaches for visualizing uncertainty information", in DODGE M., MCDERBY M., TURNER M. (eds), *Geographic Visualization*, John Wiley & Sons, Chichester, pp. 277–291, 2008.

[DER 11] DE RUNZ C., DESJARDIN E., PIANTONI F. *et al.*, "Using metadata to link uncertainty and data quality assessments", in JEREM E., REDŐ F., SZEVERÉNYI V. (eds), *On the Road to Reconstructing the Past. Computer Applications and Quantitative Methods in Archaeology (CAA). Proceedings of the 36th International Conference, Budapest, April 2–6, 2008*, Archeaeolingua, Budapest, pp. 187–191, 2011.

[DEV 06] DEVILLERS R., JEANSOULIN R., "Spatial data quality: concepts", in DEVILLERS R., JEANSOULIN R. (eds), *Fundamentals of Spatial Data Quality*, ISTE Ltd, London, pp. 31–42, 2006.

[DEV 10] DEVILLERS R., STEIN A., BÉDARD Y. *et al.*, "Thirty years of research on spatial data quality: achievements, failures and opportunities", *Transactions in GIS*, vol. 14, no. 4, pp. 387–400, 2010.

[DOU 03] DOUPNIK T.S., RICHTER M., "Interpretation of uncertainty expressions: a cross-national study", *Accounting, Organizations and Society*, vol. 28, no. 1, pp. 15–35, 2003.

[DUC 01] DUCKHAM M., MASON K., STELL J. *et al.*, "A formal approach to imperfection in geographic information", *Accounting, Organizations and Society*, vol. 25, no. 1, pp. 89–103, 2001.

[FIS 87] FISHER P.F., "The nature of soil data in GIS – error or uncertainty", in *The International Geographic Information Systems Symposium*, Arlington, 1987.

[FIS 99] FISHER P.F., "Models of uncertainty in spatial data", in LONGLEY P., GOODCHILD M.F., MAGUIRE D.J. *et al.* (eds), *Geographic Information Systems: Principles and Applications*, John Wiley & Sons, New York, vol. 1, pp. 191–205, 1999.

[FIS 03] FISHER P.F., "Data quality and uncertainty: ships passing in the night!", *2nd International Symposium on Spatial Data Quality*, Hong Kong Polytechnic University, Hong Kong, pp. 17–22, 2003.

[FIS 06] FISHER P.F., COMBER A., WADSWORTH R., "Approaches to uncertainty in spatial data", in DEVILLERS R., JEANSOULIN R. (eds), *Fundamentals of Spatial Data Quality*, ISTE Ltd, London, pp. 43–59, 2006.

[FRA 01] FRANK A., "Tiers of ontology and consistency constraints in geographic information systems", *International Journal of Geographical Information Science*, vol. 15, pp. 667–678, 2001.

[FRA 08] FRANK A., "Analysis of dependence of decision quality on data quality", *Journal of Geographical Systems*, no. 10, pp. 71–88, 2008.

[GOO 83] GOODCHILD M.F., "Accuracy and spatial resolution: critical dimensions for geoprocessing", in DOUGLAS D.H., BOYLE A.R. (eds), *Computer Assisted Cartography and Geographic Information Processing: Hope and Realism*, Canadian Cartographic Association, Ottawa, pp. 87–90, 1983.

[GOO 89] GOODCHILD M.F., "Modeling error in objects and fields", in GOODCHILD M.F., GOPAL S. (eds), *Accuracy of Spatial Databases*, Taylor and Francis, London, pp. 107–114, 1989.

[LEY 05] LEYK S., BOESCH R., WEIBEL R., "A conceptual framework for uncertainty investigation in map-based land cover change modelling", *Transactions on GIS*, no. 9, pp. 291–322, 2005.

[LON 05] LONGLEY P.A., GOODCHILD M.F., MACGUIRE D.J. *et al.*, *Geographic Information Systems and Science*, John Wiley & Sons, Hoboken, 2005.

[NAV 06a] NAVRATIL G., "Data quality for spatial planning – an ontological view", *CORP 2006*, CORP, Vienna, 2006.

[NAV 06b] NAVRATIL G., FRANK A. "What does data quality mean? An ontological framework", *AngewandteGeoinformatik (AGIT 2006)*, CORP, Wichmann, Salzburg, pp. 494–503, 2006.

[NIS 89] NISKANEN V.A., "Introduction to imprecise reasoning", in KESKINEN K. (ed.), *Uncertainty, decision making and knowledge engineering*, Society for Artificial Intelligence in Finland, pp. 11–12, 1989.

[ROB 85] ROBINSON V.B., FRANK A., "About different kinds of uncertainty in collections of spatial data", *AUTO-CARTO 7*, ASP & ACSM, Washington, DC, USA, pp. 440–449, 1985.

[SHI 09] SHI W., *Principles of Modeling Uncertainties in Spatial Data and Spatial Analyses*, CRC Press, Boca Raton, 2009.

[SME 97] SMETS P., "Uncertainty management in information systems", in MOTRO A., SMETS P. (eds), *From Needs to Solutions*, Kluwer Academic Publishers, Norwell, pp. 225–254, 1997.

[SMI 89] SMITHSON M., *Ignorance and Uncertainty: Emerging Paradigms*, Springer-Verlag, New York, 1989.

[TEI 88] TEIGEN K.H., "The language of uncertainty", *Acta Psychologica*, no. 68, pp. 27–38, 1988.

[ZHA 02] ZHANG J.X., GOODCHILD M.F., *Uncertainty in Geographical Information*, Taylor and Francis, London, 2002.

The Origins of Imperfection
in Geographic Data

3.1. Introduction

In keeping with the conceptual framework established in the previous chapter, we will focus on problems that involve imperfections in relation to internal or external quality. Knowing the sources of the imperfections of geographic information plays a significant part in characterizing its internal quality but also in handling its external quality in the areas of application in which it plays a central role. These applications may meet everyday needs, such as calculating itineraries, or complex issues, such as land management or the assessment of scenarios.

If geographic information has historically been produced by institutional or private actors, the technological developments in geomatics, computer science, or the creation of Web 2.0 have changed the way in which it is collected, analyzed, stored, distributed, and consumed. In fact, besides its technological dimension, Web 2.0 today constitutes a major social phenomenon which is blurring the line between producers and users. Thus, we refer to "produser", a portmanteau word that combines "producer" and "user" [BRU 08]. In this context, any individual who uses geographic information may act as a "sensor" [FOO 17] and take part in its modeling, collection, and analysis, questioning the historical paradigm that defined the assessment of spatial data quality, based on the division between internal and external quality. The major changes in progress are also linked to the new

Chapter written by Jean-Michel FOLLIN, Jean-François GIRRES, Ana-Maria OLTEANU-RAIMOND and David SHEEREN.

European and national policies that encourage open and freely available data (the European directive INSPIRE and its national versions, the *loi pour une République numérique*, or "law for a digital Republic" in France, which required open access to public data, etc.) as well as the emergence of spatiotemporal "Big Data", characterized among other things by uncertainty.

Therefore, today two categories of geographic information coexist: Volunteered Geographic Information[1] (VGI) [GOO 07], which refers to data willingly produced by the public, and so-called authoritative geographic information, which is produced through traditional methods by actors who are public or private, local, national, or global. Thus, several measures aimed at collecting VGI have been taken in the last 15 years or so, some of which intend to create a "frame of reference" which describes the land globally (e.g. OpenStreetMap, Wikimapia, and Google Map Maker), whereas others target specific themes or events, such as land-cover validation with LACO-Wiki [SEE 17] or the collection of data after the earthquake that hit Haiti, described in [ZOO 10]. The traditional "actors" include national mapping agencies, whose goal is to provide homogeneous topographic coverage of their territory, or such initiatives as the European program Copernicus and the French national research center THEIA, associated in particular for the production of land-cover data (OSO product) that result from processing Sentinel-2 time series.

The two categories of geographic information, namely, volunteered or authoritative, which are *a priori* very different, have the advantage of complementing each other in relation to the themes covered or the rates and scales of acquisition. However, it can be observed that the boundary between them is increasingly more porous. For example, some public actors are more and more interested in using VGI for different goals, putting forward their own platforms to interact with citizens [HAK 13, OLT 16] and to acquire or share information [JOH 13]. In this context, where the world is constantly developing on a spatial and digital level, and anyone can produce, analyze, combine, and visualize geographic information, it is no longer sufficient to focus merely on the sources of the imperfections linked to traditional mapmakers. In fact, the coproduction of geographic information, without following a rigorous collection protocol, creates significant spatiotemporal heterogeneity linked in particular to the use of various tools, sometimes with different aims, and to the lack of associated metadata.

---

1 We invite the reader to refer to the works carried out by [SEE 16] for an inventory of the various terms employed in the literature.

In this chapter, we suggest a way to categorize the various sources of imperfection in geographic information that maintains the classic distinction between different phases or processes (from the collection of data to its use), made among others by [COL 94]. We will tackle the different levels on which these processes may generate errors (at the beginning, at the end, or in relation to the resources mobilized by the process) while also taking into consideration the ways in which data are produced (traditional-volunteered).

3.2. Imperfection during the life cycle of geographic data

During its life cycle, a piece of geographic data goes through different stages, generated by a series of processes that affect it. These processes are widely different and refer to ways of manipulating data, from its acquisition stage to its representation. However, it is customary to group them into five categories [DEN 96]: abstraction, acquisition, storage, analysis, and display.

Whether it affects a piece of geographic data or not, each process may be characterized by various components – an input, an output, and resources – incorporating the material and human means and the processes implemented to carry out an action. In theory, a process that is not affected by any imperfection would generate a virtually perfect output, free from any uncertainty. In practice, there are always imperfections involved in the process, so that any output is imperfect, to a more or less significant extent.

The imperfections of geographic data may appear in each component of the process (Figure 3.1):

– the initial source (*From What?*);

– the target model (*Toward What?*);

– the measuring instrument (*With What?*);

– the procedure (*How?*);

– the operator (*By Whom?*).

We can see here the general categories of causes defined in the so-called 5M cause-effect graph [BAR 14]: the matter (the input of the process), the material (the measuring instrument with software and algorithms employed), the method (the procedure that involves the measurement), the manpower (the operator), and the milieu (which is not explicitly represented for the process but refers to its context).

Imperfections concern simultaneously the geometric dimension of a piece of geographic data and its meaning. Various sources may combine within the same process and lead to an imperfect output, which can, in turn, become the input for another process, thus spreading these imperfections.

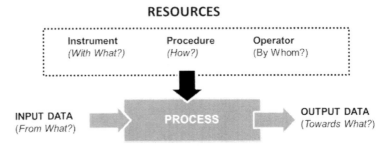

Figure 3.1. *Main components of a process related to the use of geographic data. For a color version of this figure, see www.iste.co.uk/batton/geographic1.zip*

3.3. The sources of the imperfections in a process

This section describes in more detail the sources of the imperfections that may appear in each component of a process that exploits geographic data.

3.3.1. *The target model: toward what?*

The target model refers to the expected result at the end of the application of a specific process (from acquisition to display). It simultaneously concerns raster and vector representations of geographic data. The target model is a source of imperfections when it is ill-conceived or when the characteristics of the expected result are not clearly established or too vague, leaving room for interpretation.

For vector geographic databases produced in a traditional way, the target model is regarded as the ideal product, with a "perfect" and error-free content. It is known as the "universe of discourse" or "nominal ground." As a "model", this target model constitutes an accepted abstraction of the real world, which is essentially a simplification of reality (see Chapter 2). The level of simplification varies in relation to the target uses for which a geographic database is intended (scale of representation, expected processing, etc.). It is grasped, thanks to a set of rules described in the "specifications" of the product or the collection protocols. We can distinguish between two types of specifications [VAU 97]: (1) content specifications, which describe which information must be included in the database, and (2) acquisition specifications, which establish the rules that define how the information should be represented, with the techniques and methods to employ to that end (measuring instruments, procedure, staff, etc.).

Thus, the target model of vector databases will affect the way in which the data are acquired or transformed to meet the quality goals. It makes it possible to assess the quality of the data produced by establishing the reference. Its distance from reality or degree of simplification of the actual world is not an imperfection per se. A producer requires and deals with the abstraction. The simplification of reality gives rise to imperfection when the nominal ground is not clearly established or has not even been identified. This problem may arise in the context of the traditional production of geographic data, but it is even more significant for VGI. Specifications for VGI are not always given or are often incomplete. They are general recommendations for contributors who are free to pay heed to them. The target model is much vaguer in this context, so there are more geometric or semantic imperfections affecting the data produced.

For images (especially Earth observation images), the target model also defines the expected characteristics of the product. This concerns the geometry of the images (location accuracy, level of adjustment, and inter-band superimposition), remote sensing (noise level and standardization), and resolution (spatial and spectral sampling interval, radiometric resolution, and acquisition rate). It may turn out to be difficult to assess how to adapt these characteristics to the users' needs (we refer here to the external quality of products). For example, we rarely know which signal/noise ratio of a sensor is truly adapted to each of its various uses. On the other hand, from the producer's point of view, the specifications of the images to acquire are well-defined as they allow us to calculate the dimensions of the components of the observation system (sensor, ground segment, etc.).

The imperfection of the target model characterizes the acquisition process, but it is not limited to this category. It may also arise in other processes (during the processing phase, the storage stage, etc.), when the quality or the characteristics of the expected output result are not established. For example, this is the case when an image is resampled through bilinear interpolation or to the nearest neighbor. The level of imperfection accepted for the transformed product (i.e. the gap between the initial and the final values) is rarely defined. In this respect, the target model becomes imperfect as is ill-defined. It is also imperfect since the interpolation algorithm generates imperfection, but the source this time is the instrument employed (the method – cf. section 3.3.4). Imperfection also appears when the target model is unsuitable for the piece of data produced. This problem arises particularly during the storage of data, when the generated volume exceeds the maximum size of the chosen file format (e.g. 2 Gb for the shapefile format) or when the chosen structure is not suitable (e.g. spaghetti vs. topological).

3.3.2. *The initial source: from what?*

The source constitutes the initial state of the process, be it an acquisition, an analysis, or a storage process. It corresponds in most cases to existing geographic data (maps, aerial photographs, etc.), but it may also refer to the real world, for the acquisition process. When physical terrain constitutes the initial source of a data production process, it is not possible to regard it as affected by imperfections. However, the local layout of the physical terrain may turn out to generate specific imperfections in relation to the mode of acquisition conceived. For example, the creation of a GPS point in an urban environment may be disrupted by environmental effects (e.g. multipath effects), and the acquisition of satellite images in mountainous areas runs the risk of creating more geometric distortions in the targeted product. In these two examples, the physical terrain constitutes the source of information, and the imperfections are generated by the different means of acquisition (the *With What?* and the *How?* aspects which we will focus on later).

In several scenarios (and systematically when the acquisition is not involved), processes are applied to existing sources of geographic data (raster or vector) which may be relatively old. Therefore, these initial states are affected by imperfections to different degrees (according to the means employed to generate them). When the source data are satellite or aerial images, which will be used as points of reference when digitalizing, the imperfections derive mostly from the spatial resolution of the image (correlated with the acquisition scale) and its geometric accuracy. If the images employed are classified automatically, their spectral and radiometric resolution will have an effect on the ability to discriminate objects, and it will have to be taken into consideration as a potential source of imperfection in the classification process. The pre-processing level applied to the images may also affect their quality (e.g. corrections of atmospheric effects or lack thereof).

Besides geometry, the level of semantic detail of the source also contributes to the level of imperfection at the end of the process. For example, the European land-cover database "Corine Land Cover" (CLC) may be inappropriate when mapping farm water needs. In fact, in order to choose which crop coefficient to apply, some models require a piece of data characterized by fine semantic resolution (knowledge of the crop itself), which is not included in the CLC nomenclature [BEA 11]. Relevance may also cause imperfection. A process may be carried out on obsolete source data, entailing consequences on the quality of the final product.

3.3.3. *The instrument: with what?*

The measuring instrument is regarded here as the set of means (IT, technological, algorithmic, etc.) employed to produce geographic data. The characteristics of the measuring instrument directly affect the data generated in the form of imperfections of different kinds and ranges. Quite naturally, what relates the measuring instrument to the data acquisition process is the surveying instruments (GPS, theodolites, etc.). Yet, other processes such as those that involve the analysis or storage of data are also sources of imperfections in geographic data due to the specific instruments that they employ. Thus, this section deals with the consequences of two types of instruments: first those associated with the acquisition process, then those associated with the process that involves the storage and analysis of geographic data.

According to the type of data acquisition system used, the imperfections linked to the measuring instrument may principally derive from two aspects: the quality of the instrument and the environmental conditions in which the instrument is used. If we consider the case of GPSs, the sensor market is quite significant and ranges from high-end GPS sensors (professional GPSs) based on phase measurements to GPSs intended for the general public, such as those built in smartphones and based on pseudo-range measurements. Depending on the type of sensor and the measurement taken, accuracy may vary from a few centimeters to some tens of meters [TRI 06]. However, accuracy can also vary for the same kind of sensors built with the same chip. The simultaneous use of these sensors of different brands may create highly heterogeneous traces [RAY 09].

The accuracy and the spatial resolution of the data that result from a network of sensors (like cell towers, WiFi access points, and RFID chips) depend largely on the structure of the network deployed. For example, for mobile phones, the position of a given mobile object via the system of cell towers corresponds to the receiving antenna, with a precision that ranges from some tens of meters (in urban areas) to some tens of kilometers in rural or mountainous areas. Thus, the structure of the network deployed results in quite marked spatial heterogeneity, simultaneously within the same network and between the different networks, which raises problems if joint analyses are carried out.

In geographic data acquisition processes like photogrammetric restitution or the manual digitization of aerial photographs, the measuring instrument refers to the tools that allow an operator to acquire data. For example, it refers to a mouse (or a trackball) or the screen resolution. Given the fast paces to which acquisition operators must adapt in some contexts (e.g. emergency mapping), the imprecision related to these acquisition tools also creates imperfections in the produced geographic data and depends in particular on the scale of the data acquisition.

Besides the acquisition processes, geographic data may result from the transformation of source data (e.g. contour lines) into transformed data (e.g. a raster digital terrain model). Therefore, here, the measuring instrument is associated with an analyzer rather than with a tool used to acquire data, as has been seen before. In this context, the different implementations of an algorithm or model for processing data may lead to the creation of geographic data that contain imperfections specific to the analytical process employed. For example, the generation of continuous surface of precipitations based on a series of known points that correspond to weather stations involves spatial interpolation methods that may be simple (inverse distance weighting – IDW) or more complex (kriging) and that may be equated to measuring instruments. These analytical methods generate imperfections in their implementation. Thus, the IDW algorithm may be implemented with or without the possibility of setting parameters for the value of the constraint on distance, the number of search points, and the maximum search distance. The 2.18 version of the QGIS software [QGI 18] offers no fewer than four different implementations of the IDW algorithm. Besides potentially misleading a user, this generates variable imperfections in relation to the tool employed. For LiDAR acquisition data, the volume reconstruction algorithms based on the cloud of three-dimensional points can also generate specific errors.

Even if this seems less natural than it was for the acquisition process, the storage process also employs instruments that can generate imperfections in geographic data. In fact, the storage process relies, for example, on image compression methods that may be equated to instruments that affect geographic data. Compression may generate a lack of information associated with an image. Some data formats, such as TIFF (Tagged Image File Format), make it possible to store image data without losing of quality, but this results in a significant file size. A compromise between the size of the image and the level of compression (and, therefore, of imperfection) is often sought with varying degrees of success. As a format, ECW (Enhanced Compression Wavelet) ensures less loss of information than JPEG (Joint Photographic Experts Group). The JPEG2000 format represents an alternative to the initial JPEG format that combines a high level of compression and preservation of the integrity of the image.

3.3.4. *The procedure: how?*

The way of implementing a procedure and carrying out an action can also generate imperfections. There are three causes behind these imperfections. The first is linked to the choice of an unsuitable procedure for the level of quality expected at the end of the process. In this case, the problem has to do with quality assurance[2]: the procedure should be reviewed. The second source is the method itself, which may be uncertain for a fixed procedure that has been adapted *a priori* to the requirements expected. Finally, the third source derives from a voluntary degradation of a piece of geographic data for security, confidentiality, and privacy reasons, or in a fraudulent manner.

There are several sources of imperfections related to the first origin (choosing an unsuitable procedure). This may derive from the protocol of observations during the acquisition of data (e.g. the observation period is too short for a GPS measurement), from the way in which data are acquired (e.g. the digitization of curves with three points, digitization without geometric division in a non-topological structure), or from the way to transform a dataset (e.g. passing from a projection system to another with a polynomial transformation rather than a 3D similitude for different geodesic systems; classifying an image that includes several hundred bands by using a classification algorithm that is unsuitable for such a large size).

---

2 As a reminder, this concerns the "management of quality aiming to build confidence through the compliance with the requirements for quality" (ISO 9000:2015).

In relation to the second origin (uncertain method), imperfections may result from an inappropriate configuration after a misinterpretation, the application of a method to unsuitable data (an algorithm for distance calculation applied to a dataset with non-projected geographic coordinates), or imprecisions inherent in the operation carried out (e.g. changing the pixel values of an image by resampling after a reprojection; uncertainty about interpolated values). In the latter case, the uncertainty may be limited, but it is not always possible to avoid.

Finally, the procedure may also create some imperfection in a deliberate manner. Thus, when an organization degrades a piece of geographic data before disseminating it, we refer to controlled uncertainty [FIS 99]. For example, for confidentiality reasons, INSEE disseminates the tax revenues of households situated in 200 m grids. To prevent the precise identification of the individuals in question, small-size grids (those that include fewer than 11 households) are grouped in bigger rectangles, so that imperfection is created. This controlled uncertainty may also be motivated by the aim to protect our heritage or the environment (e.g. the introduction of systematic or random errors in the location of nest sites of species of endangered birds), by national security issues (e.g. the exact location of stations related to the quality of groundwater is not disclosed to the general public on the portal ADES[3] for displaying scales smaller than 1/100,000), or by privacy issues (e.g. blurring faces in recordings, combining the commuting routes that result from town surveys, anonymizing usernames, etc.).

If we consider VGI, a malicious contributor can deliberately degrade geographic data. In this case, we refer to vandalism [BAL 14]. Once again, there may be various reasons: giving a fanciful or artistic dimension to data, highlighting a personal vision of land-use planning, or simply causing harm.

Unlike the aforementioned cases, the procedure may also be used to limit the data imperfection. Thus, taking multiple measurements – enabled by a collaborative approach – which occasionally generates very significant volumes of data ("Big Data"), makes it possible to correct the uncertainty in the data created by the "produsers". For example, by combining several measurements of coastlines taken by different contributors at different times with mainstream GPSs (e.g. data of limited planimetric accuracy and whose acquisition protocol varies from person to person), it is possible to obtain an acceptable approximation of the studied phenomenon, with a temporal and

---

3 Groundwater national portal.

spatial coverage that is potentially more thorough than that obtained by more traditional means (through LiDAR surveys, photogrammetry, or topography) [PON 17].

3.3.5. *The operator: by whom?*

As has been pointed out before, the producers of geographic data are changing with the development of Web 2.0 technologies and the success of collaborative initiatives. The classic production operator is being joined by a voluntary and involuntary operator, whether amateur or not ("produser").

The role of classic producers involves generating data homogeneously and exhaustively on a territorial scale. This is the case for mapping institutes such as the IGN (topographic data), INSEE (socioeconomic data), the Directorate-General for Taxation (Land Registry), as well as other private and public actors. However, citizens today take part in the production of geographic data by contributing to collaborative platforms. They produce data willingly through applications or sharing devices (e.g. geolocated tweets or pictures) or without being aware, through log systems whose primary goal is to improve service quality. In the latter scenario, data are stored by the owners of services, such as telephone companies, transport actors (Vélib, métro), energy actors, banks, and so on, without informing users beforehand. These new types of data, which raise confidentiality issues, also play a part in enriching traditional data, which in some areas fall short, for example, in spatial mobility or epidemiology.

Whether professional or voluntary, an operator can create imperfection. In a classic procedure in which an operator follows a collection protocol and well-defined and detailed specifications, imperfection may be of a cognitive kind, resulting in a different assessment of an aspect (e.g. a metro station is represented by more than two points if it is an important hub; here the notion of importance is open to interpretation) or specification (e.g. when considering the rule "buildings smaller than 20 use sq. m. are excluded from the database", an operator may decide to include an edifice that is only slightly smaller). The imperfections that derive from voluntary operators may be created by a lack of experience (e.g. an operator who is not familiar with land-cover data). A voluntary action also creates various problems related to spatial exhaustiveness (e.g. data are generally more numerous in urban areas than in rural ones) [MA 15].

3.4. Examples of sources of imperfection in different processes

After introducing the various sources of imperfection in the previous sections, in this part, we examine three examples by establishing processes and the components that can create imperfection affecting the final result.

EXAMPLE 3.1.– *Land-cover mapping by classification of satellite images.*

This example illustrates the sources of imperfection in a process where land-cover is mapped by classifying satellite images. In this scenario, illustrated in Figure 3.2, some researchers in agronomy focus on the development of farming practices on survey land, which is situated in West Africa and mostly unmapped. In order to gain some basic knowledge, the researchers decide to draw a land-cover map based on freely available satellite data and land surveys. Afterward, it will be possible to update this land-cover map regularly in order to study the development of farming practices.

The target model corresponds to a land-cover polygonal covering layer based on six classes (woodland, farmland, grassland, bare soil, urbanized areas, and surface water) which can be displayed on a scale that ranges between 1:100,000 and 1:250,000. The imprecision of the target model, caused by the choice of land-cover classification and the semantic similarity between certain concepts, constitutes the first source of imperfection that may lead to spectral confusions between classes.

The initial data source is an optical satellite image taken by Sentinel-2, whose spatial resolution is 10 m, by exploiting channels in the visible range (red, green, blue) and in the near infrared. The Sentinel-2 image is processed at Level 2A, namely, in orthorectified geometry and surface reflectance after atmospheric corrections. Therefore, the raw image has already been transformed several times before it gets integrated into the classification procedure. Despite these transformations, this image inherently has some limitations (spatial, spectral, and radiometric resolution) which will affect the quality of the final result.

In addition to the satellite data, the agronomists have identified in the field GPS points that correspond to each type of land cover and that will be used as a learning sample for the image classification procedure. These GPS points are affected by the imperfections associated with the acquisition through GNSS surveys (quality of the sensor, environmental conditions, etc.).

To draw the land-cover map, a maximum likelihood algorithm (a Gaussian mixture model) is used to carry out a supervised pixel-based classification (i.e. without preliminary segmentation of the image). This classification approach means to, in advance, determine the training areas in the image around the GPS points found in the field. These training areas are manually digitized, and the choices related to the creation of these learning samples (size by class, spatial distribution of the areas, etc.) can significantly affect the results of the final classification. Based on this sample, 70% of the areas are employed to classify the image, and the remaining 30% are used to validate the classification. Once the classification procedure is over, a majority filter is used on the output image (with a 3 × 3 window) to eliminate the isolated pixels regarded as noise. Finally, the image is vectorized (and smoothed to remove the pixel effect) in order to create the land-cover polygonal covering.

The image is classified thanks to a classic satellite image processing program, and training areas are identified with GIS software and through photointerpretation. The implementation of these various methods (classification, filtering, and vectorization) through these programs may be regarded as a source of imperfections.

Finally, the overall image classification procedure is carried out by some researchers in agronomy, who have good knowledge of the land but do not consider themselves as experts in geographic information acquisition and processing. It is important to regard this "thematic" heritage as a source of potential subjectivity, which affects the land-cover mapping process, especially through the choice of classification or training areas.

Finally, the land-cover map is drawn. The correspondence between the map and the validation sample is 82%, despite the measures taken when sampling and validating the training areas. This means that 18% of the training areas are incorrectly classified. This example aptly demonstrates that besides the imperfection inherent in the source data, the image classification process incorporates various resources (instrument, operator, and procedure) which contribute to the global imperfection of the land-cover data produced.

RESOURCES

Instrument	Procedure	Operator
GPS-Sensor	Choice of a nomenclature	Agronomist
GIS and Remote Sensing software	Digitizing of training areas	Researcher
Algo: maximum likelihood	Supervised classification	
Algo: polygonization	Post-processing: filtering and vectorization	

Image SENTINEL-2A
GPS Points → **IMAGE CLASSIFICATION** → **Land Cover Map**

Figure 3.2. *Sources of imperfection in the process involving the classification of a satellite image. For a color version of this figure, see www.iste.co.uk/batton/geographic1.zip*

EXAMPLE 3.2.– *Manual vectorization of cadastral maps carried out by an operator.*

This example describes how some sources of imperfections can emerge in the processes related to the vector data produced by so-called "traditional" actors (see Figure 3.3). More precisely, to explain our point, we will use as an example the hypothetical manual vectorization of scanned cadastral maps (which derive from a renovation planned as part of an "update"), a task carried out by a certified provider on behalf of a tax office.

The target model of the vectorization corresponds to a layer of polygons that represent the plots and respect a given number of topological rules like "there can be no spatial overlap or gap between two adjacent plots". However, the model is affected by some uncertainty, as the acquisition specifications do not indicate how to draw the outline of the plots, given that in the original document they were traced with thick lines, which are represented by a wide multipixel line in the digitized document. Thus, this remains open to interpretation, as the operator may choose to rely on the line or on one of the two edges of the line.

The scanned paper document combines bad graphical quality (linked to wear and tear and the conservation conditions) with low geometric quality. This is a simple implementation of the Napoleonic plan dating back to the beginning of the 19th century. Therefore, it presents the same georeferencing shortcomings inherent in the measuring technologies of the period. Furthermore, the digitization process itself has created imperfection during the scanning phase. The operator will use a suitable vectorization tool, but he or she will not always choose the topological editing option (vertex snapping), thus generating invalid overlap areas between adjacent plots. An inexperienced user will occasionally make assessment errors, mistaking the boundaries of buildings with those of plots.

In the aforementioned example, errors appear in each component of the "manual vectorization" process (except for the choice of tool). These errors combine, producing imperfect vector data at the end of the process. This imperfection will spread and complement that involved in the following processes; for example, a georeferencing process, which itself involves errors (choosing the wrong repositioning function and/or using an insufficient number of control points).

RESOURCES

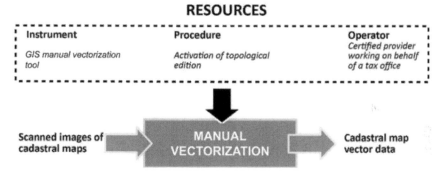

Figure 3.3. *Sources of imperfections in a manual vectorization process. For a color version of this figure, see www.iste.co.uk/batton/geographic1.zip*

EXAMPLE 3.3– *The layouts of ski pistes in a mountain area acquired by various volunteers.*

In order to draw ski maps or keep them updated, the managers of ski areas need to know the boundaries of ski resorts. Access to this information is not included in either authoritative data or VGI. Thus, the managers of a ski area in the Alps have decided to estimate these boundaries through spatial analysis based on various sources of geographic data. Once a ski resort has been identified, the need to obtain the layouts of the ski pistes has been identified. Consequently, the managers have decided to organize a map-party to collect the layouts of the pistes that belong to their ski area.

Thus, several volunteers with GPS sensors have divided up the territory to collect data. This hypothetical scenario is illustrated in Figure 3.4.

The target model for the acquisition of the layouts corresponds to a layer of shelves. No detailed specifications have been set down, and there is only a document that gives some recommendations about the procedure (acquisition rate, types of tools, etc.). However, the recommendations do not mention that off-ski pistes have to be collected too. Some volunteers have done so, whereas others have not. Thus, this has resulted in a lack of exhaustiveness in the form of a gap in the final set of pistes.

The chosen tool, namely, GPS sensors, is suitable. On the other hand, each volunteer has his or her own GPS (built in his or her mobile phone or smartwatch, mainstream or professional GPSs). Therefore, this results in pistes whose location accuracy varies. For pistes in forested areas, the effect of the vegetation cover, regardless of the quality of the GPS, leads to aberrant points whose precision falls outside the range allowed.

With regard to the procedure, despite the recommendations that suggested a 2 min GPS acquisition rate, some volunteers have chosen to collect data less frequently (from every 5 to 10 min), whereas others have respected the rule but collected data about the cross-country pistes on a bicycle. This leads to significant heterogeneity between the pistes and less precise segments which connect two consecutive points.

When storing the traces of pistes, a volunteer forgot to tick the box of the option "Add Timestamps". This manipulation error has generated a lack of completeness because some points do not have a timestamp.

As has been pointed out before, these errors combine and are added to those of the following processes. For example, all the pistes collected in GPX format will then be transformed in the Lambert 93 system so that they can be cross-referenced with the other geographic data available (the buildings and ski-lifts of the IGN BDTOPO database). Due to the low levels of precision, the zones marking the ski resorts areas, calculated by cross-referencing the aforementioned data, have been overestimated. On the maps drawn, it is possible to see that some GPS tracks pass over houses.

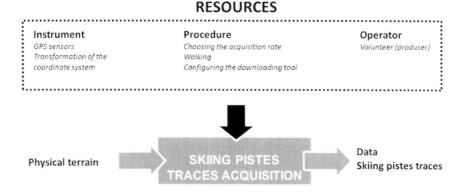

Figure 3.4. *Sources of imperfections in a process in which data about ski pistes is collaboratively collected. For a color version of this figure, see www.iste.co.uk/batton/geographic1.zip*

3.5. Conclusion

In this chapter, we have shown through which components (initial source, target model, measuring tool, procedure, and operator) imperfections may find their way into the five classic processes that characterize the life cycle of geographic data (the famous five As). We have demonstrated that these imperfections concern various dimensions (semantic, geometric, and temporal) and different types (vector, raster) of geographic data. We have then used three examples to illustrate how imperfections can emerge and combine with one another during the manipulation of geographic data: a researcher who classifies satellite images, a "traditional" operator who manually vectorizes land-register plates, and the collaborative collection of data about ski pistes. It follows that imperfection is inevitable and derives from a large number of sources, regardless of the process applied to the geographic data. This applies even more to the current context, which is characterized by the emergence of new types of data (VGI, Big Data, and open data) that include uncertainty among their most prominent features.

Imperfection does not prevent the use of data, but some precautions must be taken to ensure that the data employed are adapted to the intended application and the standard expected at the end of the process. In this respect, metadata plays a central role. It provides a user with information about the provenance of the data, so that it becomes possible to assess its relevance more accurately, in addition to quality indicators [BOI 08]. It also makes it easier to disseminate the data, and it facilitates its interoperability. Several norms suggest structuring metadata by using different categories (e.g. quality, mode, reference, reference system, etc.). However, in the age of open data, it is becoming crucial, on the one hand, to be able to enrich and develop the types of metadata and, on the other hand, to define metadata for the data resulting from any process. If traditionally it was only a data producer who defined, knew, and verified the coherence of metadata, it is now important that this data can be checked by any user. Therefore, paying more attention to semantic distinctions could improve data usability. If metadata is traditionally expressed in relation to resources (e.g. a vector geographic dataset and a classification), occasionally it may become necessary to define it in more detail. For example, when dealing with vector geographic data, it would be useful to provide for each geographic object some quality indicators, some information about the sensor or the algorithm used and so on. In a given context, this would make it possible to use only a sample of the dataset which meets the requirements in question. Generally, this would improve our way of controlling and understanding the imperfections linked to these processes and the bias that they may generate.

3.6. References

[BAL 14] BALLATORE A., "Defacing the map: cartographic vandalism in the digital commons", *The Cartographic Journal*, vol. 51, no. 3, pp. 214–224, available at: http://dx.doi.org/10.1179/1743277414y.0000000085, 2014.

[BAR 14] BARSALOU M.A., *Root Cause Analysis: a Step-by-Step Guide to Using the Right Tool at the Right Time*, CRC Press, Boca Raton, available at: https://www.taylorfrancis.com/books/9781482258806, 2014.

[BEA 11] BEAUFILS M., FOLLIN J.-M., "Toward a quality aware SDI to assess agricultural water consumption", *Conference EnviroInfo 2011 Innovations in Sharing Environmental Observation and Information*, JRC-Ispra, Italy, 5–7 October 2011.

[BOI 08] BOIN A.T., HUNTER G.J., "What communicates quality to the spatial data consumer?", in STEIN A., BIJKER W., SHI W. (eds), *Quality Aspects in Spatial Data Mining*, CRC Press, Boca Raton, 2008.

[BRU 08] BRUNS A., *Blogs, Wikipedia, Second Life and Beyond: From Production to Produsage*, Peter Lang, New York, 2008.

[COL 94] COLLINS F., SMITH J., "Taxonomy for error in GIS", in *Proceedings of the International Symposium on the Spatial Accuracy of Natural Resource Data Bases*, ASPRS, pp. 1–7, 1994.

[DEN 96] DENÈGRE J., SALGÉ F., *Les Systèmes d'information géographique*, PUF, que sais-je?, no. 1322, 1996.

[GIR 10] GIRRES J.-F., TOUYA G., "Quality assessment of the French OpenStreetMap dataset", *Transactions in GIS*, vol. 14, no. 4, pp. 435–459, 2010.

[GOO 07] GOODCHILD M.F., "Citizens as sensors: the world of volunteered geography", *GeoJournal*, vol. 69, no. 4, pp. 211–221, available at: doi.org/10.1007/s10708-007-9111-y, 2007.

[FIS 99] FISHER P.F., "Models of uncertainty in spatial data", *Geographical Information Systems*, vol. 1, pp. 191–205, 1999.

[FOO 17] FOODY G., SEE L., FRITZ S. *et al.*, *Mapping and the Citizen Sensor*, Ubiquity Press Ltd, London, doi: 10.5334/bbf, 2017.

[HAK 13] HAKLAY M., "Citizen science and volunteered geographic information: overview and typology of participation", in SUI D., ELWOOD S., GOODCHILD M. (eds), *Crowdsourcing Geographic Knowledge*, Springer, Dordrecht, pp. 105–122, 2013.

[JOH 13] JOHNSON P., SIEBER R., "Situating the adoption of VGI by government", in SUI D., ELWOOD S., GOODCHILD M. (eds), *Crowdsourcing Geographic Knowledge*, Springer, Dordrecht, The Netherlands, 2013.

[MA 15] MA D., SANDBERG M., JIANG B., "Characterizing the heterogeneity of the OpenStreetMap data and community", ISPRS International Journal of Geo-Information, vol. 4, pp. 535–550, doi:10.3390/ijgi4020535, 2015.

[OLT 16] OLTEANU-RAIMOND A.-M., HART G., TOUYA G. *et al.*, "The scale of VGI in map production: a perspective of European National Mapping Agencies", *Transactions in GIS*, vol. 21, no. 1, pp. 74–90, doi:10.1111/tgis.12189, 2016.

[PON 17] PONS F., MOULIN C., TRMAL C. *et al.*, "Rivages, devenez un acteur du littoral!" *Sign@ture no. 63, CEREMA*, pp. 4–8, June 2017.

[QGI 18] QGIS DEVELOPMENT TEAM, "QGIS Geographic Information System", Open Source Geospatial Foundation Project, available at: http://qgis.osgeo.org, 2018.

[RAY 09] RAY C., "Dispositifs mobiles, ubiquité: Mobilité, contexte et localisation", *Ecole d'été MAGIS*, available at: https://www.youscribe.com/catalogue/documents/education/cours/cours-3-dispositifs-mobiles-ubiquite-1392714, Aussois, France, 7–11 September 2009.

[SEE 16] SEE L., MOONEY P., FOODY G. *et al.*, "Crowdsourcing, citizen science or volunteered geographic information? The current state of crowdsourced geographic information", *ISPRS International Journal of Geo-Information*, vol. 5, no. 5, p. 55, doi:10.3390/ijgi5050055, 2016.

[SEE 17] SEE L., LASO BAYAS J.-C., SCHEPASCHENKO D. *et al.*, "LACO-Wiki: a new online land cover validation tool demonstrated using GlobeLand30 for Kenya", *Remote Sensing*, vol. 9, p. 754, doi:10.3390/rs9070754, 2017.

[TRI 06] TRIMBLE NAVIGATION LIMITED, "Differentiating between recreational and professional grade GPS receivers", available at: http://www. gsiworks.com/Recreational%20Versus%20Professional%20GPS.pdf, 2006.

[VAU 97] VAUGLIN F., Modèle statistique des imprécisions géométriques des objets géographiques linéaires, PhD thesis, Université Marne-la-Vallée, 1997.

[WIE 16] WIENER P., STEIN M., SEEBACHER D. et al., "BigGIS: a continuous refinement approach to master heterogeneity and uncertainty in spatio-temporal big data", in Proceedings of the 24th ACM SIGSPATIAL International Conference on Advances in Geographic Information Systems, p. 8, 2016.

[ZOO 10] ZOOK M., GRAHAM M., SHELTON T. et al., "Volunteered geographic information and crowdsourcing disaster relief: a case study of the Haitian earthquake", World Medical & Health Policy, vol. 2, no. 2, pp. 7–33, 2010.

Integrity and Trust of Geographic Information

4.1. Introduction

Uncertainty, like data quality, can be of different types, and be described, formalized, and considered in decision-making processes in various ways. While many questions related to the uncertainty and quality of geographic information can be traced back to conventional mapping practices (see examples in previous chapters), the processes involving the production and dissemination of information at present is much more complex than in the past. Thus, whereas national mapping agencies may guarantee the production of maps of quality, the highly widespread and dynamic nature of some current data, such as measurements collected by sensor networks, can result in an assessment of quality that differs widely from the traditional methods developed in mapping.

In this chapter, we present the concepts of integrity and trust in the context of the assessment of spatial data quality. We describe approaches that can be used to assess the internal and external quality of geolocated information produced by mobile objects. The first step, a bottom-up approach, suggests assessing the integrity of information (an internal quality element) based on the database structure. The second step, a top-down approach, suggests assessing the trust (an external quality element) that should be given to information based on the measures that can be applied to a dataset.

Chapter written by Clément IPHAR, Benjamin COSTÉ, Aldo NAPOLI, Cyril RAY and Rodolphe DEVILLERS.

Taking the example of geolocation data, in particular, in the context of maritime navigation, we demonstrate how these concepts and methods may be used to define the integrity and trust of the data produced by a vessel monitoring system. Characterizing the integrity and trust of geographic information makes it possible to provide better information about the uncertainty of the data used in decision-making processes in maritime safety, thus minimizing the risks of improper uses.

4.2. The notions of quality

4.2.1. *Data quality and its dimensions*

Any geographic dataset is a simplified and hence imperfect representation of reality, which is affected by various quality problems. Data quality is generally described from two different perspectives: (1) internal quality, which is the quality of the product/dataset as conceived by a producer, and (2) external quality, which is generally regarded as being the fitness for use.

Various authors (e.g. [PIE 11, WAN 96]) have put forward criteria/ indicators/dimensions that can describe the data quality. Since the 1980s, various groups have described and then standardized internal quality, before the ISO (International Organization for Standardization) standardized it on an international level. The ISO standards identify elements that must be qualified or quantified and then documented when a data producer desires to comply with the given standard (e.g. ISO 19157)[1]. These criteria include spatial accuracy, attribute accuracy, temporal accuracy, completeness, and logical consistency (see the ISO standards for a complete list of quality elements and sub-elements). Assessing internal quality usually implies comparing the dataset produced with a dataset the data producer would have provided in an ideal context (without making mistakes). Such an ideal dataset is called "universe of discourse", "*nominal ground*", or "ground truth".

It is harder to describe external quality in only one way, as no consensus has been reached and no international standardization has been carried out. However, authors have suggested criteria that can describe it, including Wang and Strong's quality dimensions [WAN 96], which are described by Pierkot [PIE 10]:

---

1 https://www.iso.org/obp/ui/fr/#iso:std:iso:19157:ed-1:v1:fr.

– Intrinsic quality: it establishes the reliability, precision, objectivity, and reputation of data according to a user.

– Contextual quality: it verifies whether data are suitable (relevance, added value) and sufficient (completeness, data volume) for the use expected.

– Representational quality: for the notions of data interoperability and interpretability.

– Data accessibility and security.

Other criteria for describing external data quality, including up-to-dateness, reliability, reputation, accessibility, relevance, or interpretability, have been put forward [PIE 10]. These criteria make it possible to assess the diversity of the factors that affect the use of data in a specific context.

Generally, internal quality is the intrinsic quality of a dataset established through rules. It is an absolute technical quality. External quality is harder to assess, due to multiple and varied user needs, the link between data and their use, problems related to data providers, and users' expectations. Therefore, external quality is often relative, associated with specific usages and with the ability of a dataset to meet a specific need.

4.2.2. Assessing data quality

Following on from Wang *et al.* [WAN 95], a model for assessing data quality must consider whether data are original or of a modified/intermediate version. Certifications and inspections can also improve authenticity and build trust in data.

The transition from analog to digital media may make it difficult to assess data quality [GER 03]. Unlike traditional data, which exist on a physical medium (e.g. a map), digital media do not age in appearance, preventing users from judging certain criteria that could provide information about data quality, especially its obsolescence. In addition, the distributed data-production context may prevent users from verbally communicating with one another and sharing information about the quality of the data transmitted. This difficulty may entail potential risks, as users can be led to use an inappropriate dataset without being aware of its degree of fitness for use. This is a significant problem for the assessment of the quality of the work carried out using these datasets because the final quality of the work is a function of the quality of the original data.

The assessment of external quality is made by the final users, who will forge their opinion based on their intuition, using their experience, the information available about the datasets (e.g. metadata), and other criteria which may influence their judgment (e.g. data availability, costs, the type of use, and possible consequences).

Data quality may be partially associated with problems caused by heterogeneous data representations, something that can lead to data being misinterpreted. Given that data semantics is also heterogeneous, quality problems affecting the data ensue. When the same piece of information is presented in various ways in the same database, a data quality indicator will tend to decrease when these databases are combined, owing to differences in semantics used to represent similar data in the datasets to be combined. This is the case even when the intrinsic value of the data is the same.

4.2.3. *Problems linked to data of poor quality*

Poor data quality may increase risks of misuse and, in some cases, result in catastrophes. For example, error rates of 30%, which may go up to 75%, are estimated [FIS 01] to be common in industrial databases. Given the scarcity of datasets of near-perfect quality, users are often faced with a decision that requires managing the risk potentially linked to the use of imperfect data. Agumya and Hunter [AGU 98], for example, present various mechanisms that can be implemented to reduce, avoid, or accept residual use risks (i.e. risks that cannot be avoided). When users deal with imperfect data, they tend to reduce the uncertainty of the information, the extent of losses in case of an unfavorable event, and the degree of use of these data, or to increase the acceptable risk [AGU 98].

4.3. Internal quality and integrity

Geographic information can, in the present time, be easily produced, disseminated, and used by professionals and the general public alike. In many cases, the quality of this information is not assessed. Therefore, imperfect data spread as easily as good data, creating risks of misuse. After introducing the concept of integrity, we present a method for assessing the integrity of data based on the structure of the data produced and disseminated by a geolocation system. Such an approach may be suitable for other types of geographic information.

4.3.1. *The concept of integrity*

The concept of integrity is linked to logical consistency, which is used to describe the internal quality of geographic data. It is also related to the concept of data anomaly, which may propagate to other information systems.

[WAN 10] regards consistency as a linear measurement of the dependence of two processes. A value of 0 means that a process or data cannot be used to predict the other linearly. On the other hand, a value of 1 suggests a process or data that allow a total linear prediction of the other. A non-null value defines the degree of association between the two values.

This definition of consistency (sometimes referred to as coherence) allows us to define the concept of integrity as it is understood between values that derive from different data fields. It should be pointed out that all geographic data can be affected by integrity problems. Within the wide variety of geographic data, the data produced by modern geolocations systems (e.g. the GPS of a smartphone) aptly illustrate common integrity problems. These data, which are collaborative and often uncontrolled, are typically structured as messages that convey multiple pieces of information contained in fields and communicated at variable rates. Besides, given the heterogeneous nature of the messages and fields of these data, the information can be analyzed in different ways. Therefore, the following sections aim to discuss integrity through the lens of such data.

The concept of data integrity is intrinsically related to the concepts of consistency and anomaly. Thus, assessing data aims to detect any data transmitted by the geolocation system that does not meet specific expectations. Because of the growing volume of data produced by positioning systems, some works have focused on the detection of geolocation anomalies [LAX 11]. We can identify three broad categories of anomalies that apply to data analysis [CHA 09]:

– Individual anomalies: specific data are found to be anomalous when compared to the rest of the data (e.g. a land elevation reaching 15,000 m).

– Collective anomalies: individual data in a larger set of data may seem normal when looked at individually, but may appear abnormal when combined and compared with each other (e.g. the coordinates of adjacent sea buoys may be consistent when considered one by one but, when compared, a specific buoy may seem to move rapidly, while all the others did not move, so that an anomaly seems present).

– Contextual or conditional anomalies: individual data can be found to be abnormal when compared to its context (e.g. a sub-zero temperature at 12 pm in the summer on the French Riviera).

An anomaly propagated by a geolocation system results either from an accident (error) or from an intentional and malicious act (the author of the anomaly has falsified the data, or an actor outside the system has hacked the device). Accidental erroneous information is regarded as false, incomplete, or impossible, physically or based on a standard. Falsification results from a voluntary and malicious act that aims to degrade the information transmitted by modifying a genuine value, stopping the information flow willingly, or impersonating the data producer.

Analyzing these anomalies requires then to distinguish between the different interactions with the system in order to identify, prioritize, and pre-empt the associated risks. The following section introduces an analytical approach designed for detecting anomalies due to unintentional or malicious acts and conveyed in the messages sent by a geolocation system. This so-called bottom-up approach relies on the structure of the data to analyze.

4.3.2. Analyzing data integrity

Geolocation systems send one or more types of messages which together constitute time series data. Data may be conveyed by several messages and also depend on other data. Thus, this structure makes it possible to guide the processes whereby integrity is assessed. We introduce an approach based on four complementary and successive steps that allow us to analyze the integrity of geolocation data (Figure 4.1). This approach is meant to be generic and suitable for all types of geolocation systems that send one or more types of messages and contain one or more fields. The first three steps can be applied to all geolocation systems. The fourth one is designed for systems that send messages of different types (e.g. rescue alert messages and messages related to the navigation and position of a vessel).

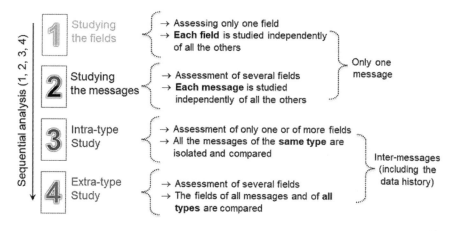

Figure 4.1. *A four-step analysis of integrity. For a color version of this figure, see www.iste.co.uk/batton/geographic1.zip*

4.3.2.1. *Studying the fields*

The first step, also known as first-order analysis, involves monitoring the integrity of each field considered individually for each message. Thus, the goal is to compare the value found in a field (which may be static or dynamic, manually entered or obtained by a sensor) with: (1) the technical specifications of the system, which may define possible and forbidden values, and (2) the geographic specifications of the environment in which the geolocation system develops. For example, a longitude of 200°W is not consistent with the technical specifications of a GPS (which allows a maximum of 180 W). Similarly, latitude/longitude coordinates that correspond to a land area are not consistent with the geographic specifications of a sea buoy. Thus, it is important to assess data consistency in relation to the technical device employed and its context.

4.3.2.2. *Studying the messages*

The second step of the analysis, also known as second-order analysis, corresponds to the assessment of the integrity of data in the same message. Thus, the goal of this analysis is to assess the integrity of a field value compared to the values of the other fields in order to detect impossible or inconsistent combinations. For example, the dew point value, which is calculated based on relative humidity and temperature, must be kept within the values of these two parameters. The pieces of information conveyed in a message must then be kept within one another.

4.3.2.3. *Intra-type study*

The third step of the analysis, also known as third-order analysis, involves comparing several messages of the same kind to identify discrepancies between the values of one or more fields in a time series of messages. For example, in this way, it is possible to analyze changes in the position or speed of a GPS transmitter and detect aberrations like accelerations or signal jumps which cannot occur in real life. Thus, messages of the same type must convey the same information or the same pieces of information in keeping with one another.

4.3.2.4. *Extra-type study*

Finally, a last type of analysis, called fourth-order analysis, involves examining messages of different kinds by comparing their information in order to extract discrepancies between the values of one or several fields in a time series. These analyses can detect discrepancies that remained unidentified during the third stage, which only considers the information contained in the same type of message. For example, if a vessel sends information in a message about a fishing activity which is not in keeping with its speed and position, which are sent in another message, this information will be updated during this last phase. Therefore, various messages must convey consistent information.

This analysis, which measures integrity, can identify some indicators of the information conveyed by the various geolocation messages. The combined indicators associated with complementary databases, such as environmental or meteorological data, can give warnings linked in particular to the integrity of information or the context (e.g. the environment, the state of the device). The combined warnings can then indicate the likeliest risk scenarios.

4.4. External quality and trust

The various disruptions that can alter the confidentiality, integrity, availability, and even the traceability of geographic information raise questions about the trust a human being or a computer system may have in data. This is an element often associated with external data quality.

4.4.1. *Definitions of trust*

Various authors have attempted to define and even model trust in several fields [BLO 97, MCK 00]. The models put forward in economics generally favor the cooperation among agents (e.g. companies, banks, and advisors) who "work and act together on a task, and share the profits or benefits from doing so" [MAR 94]. Through the link between the concepts of cooperation and trust, Demolombe [DEM 01] expanded these models with the concept of sincerity. Indeed, the author points out that Individual A can have trust in Individual B only if B is sincere from A's viewpoint. More clearly, B should not conceal information that is important for A [LOR 08]. However, it is perhaps not in B's interest to be sincere. Thus, sincerity allows us to take into consideration how trust depends on everyone's objectives or interests. If A and B have opposite interests, then each will naturally be suspicious of the other. In this case, cooperation will be nearly impossible.

To overcome the shortcomings of the previous definitions, Grandison and Sloman [GRA 00] have defined trust as "the firm belief in the competence of an entity to act dependably, securely, and reliably within a specified context". A definition in which the notion of competence is expressed as "the ability of an entity to perform the functions expected of it". Founding trust on competence, this definition is suitable for heterogeneous information sources (humans, sensors, and machines). Even more recently, the emergence and rapid proliferation of sensors of all kinds that contribute to information systems (especially mobile phones) are raising new questions about the expression of trust in the collected and transmitted information. In fact, entities (humans, systems, or sensors) are linked to the information they send [JOU 14]. Thus, some of their features (e.g. reliability, trust, and competence) influence the information produced. For example, it is possible to assess certain properties of a source from the measurement of some information properties (e.g. quality, trust, and credibility). The opposite is also true: trust in information depends on the trust in the entity. Paglieri *et al.* [PAG 14] analyze this link and establish trust in an entity as the expected quality of information. Based on their analysis, a higher degree of trust in an entity corresponds to information of higher quality. When measuring the quality of information, trust in an entity is adapted as it affects two of the entity's features: competence and sincerity. These characteristics are based on Demolombe's model [DEM 01]. They are not the only elements that characterize the behavior of an entity, but Liu and Williams [LIU 02] have demonstrated that other criteria (e.g. vigilance and cooperation) can be reduced to these two.

Hartmann and Boyens [HAR 01] point out that "when we gather information from less than fully reliable sources, then the more coherent the story that materializes is, the more confident we may be". Thus, if some information is partly coherent and partly contradictory, the trust in the information produced based on the dataset will depend on the trust we place in the various sources.

Trust must take into account the potential malice of an information source that willingly alters the data and their integrity. However, an entity may also make mistakes (e.g. by accidentally providing inaccurate information). Therefore, in order to provide different models for an entity's accidental errors and intentional tampering, a relevant trust model should rely at least on the notions of competence and sincerity [COS 16].

4.4.2. Measuring trust

Below, we describe competence, sincerity, and trust measures for data entities related to sensors (e.g. a GPS). In this context, these entities are data sources that constitute the inputs of an information system: they perceive the environment of the system and supply the other entities with their measurements. Therefore, any component of the system receives, whether directly or not, information derived from one or more sources. Thus, once the trust of these sources has been measured, the value may be propagated to any other component (depending on a source). Thus, the trust level that may be assigned to the components depends on that of the sources.

The trust measures detailed in this section consider trust as a function of competence and sincerity, which evolve over time [LIU 02, PAG 14]. These measures are built by considering two hypotheses: first, a system does not include elements that are faulty or work in degraded mode; second, each element of the system complies with the technical specifications necessary for its functioning. More clearly, the intrinsic characteristics of an element of the system do not change over time. Thus, the components do not wear down as time goes by.

4.4.2.1. Measuring competence

Competence may be measured and represented formally. For example, let us consider "sensor" types of sources that take digital measurements (one-dimensional signals). Since the measurement is not perfect, these information sources may be modeled using random processes where the inaccuracy of the measurement of a signal (process $X(t)$) is modeled as the addition of a Gaussian noise $b(t)$ to the situation observed. The information provided by the sensors is then modeled through an observation augmented by a standard normal distribution random noise $N(0, \sigma)$ [COS 17].

Section 4.4.1 defines the competence *Comp* of an entity based on its "ability to perform the functions expected of it". When a source is considered, competence depends on the imprecision of its measurement. This is an observation of reality that is affected by errors. In fact, a measurement can be more or less precise and reflect reality more or less accurately. When an ideal or a perfect source is considered, a measurement is strictly equal to the actual value of an observation ($I(t) = X(t)$). On the contrary, a significant imprecision results in a measurement that is decorrelated from the environment. Thus, a source is regarded as all the more competent as it performs its function by providing a measurement that is as close as possible to the actual observation. We have just pointed out various constraints on competence measure:

– The competence of a source must be as high as possible when the inaccuracy is minimal (in case of an ideal source: *Comp* = 1).

– When inaccuracy is at its highest, competence reaches its minimum levels.

– We also assume that the competence of a source decreases in relation to its inaccuracy.

– Considering two sources, the more competent one is the more precise one. Its measurement is the best or most accurate representation.

Based on this information source model, in which inaccuracy corresponds to the addition of a Gaussian noise $b(t)$ with distribution $N(0, \sigma)$, with a standard deviation σ, we will look for a competence measure f_c so that:

$$\text{Comp} = f_c(b) = f_c(\sigma) \text{ where } b \text{ is centered and } f_c(\sigma) \in [0; 1] \qquad [4.1]$$

Assuming a perfect source, the level of competence is at its maximum, i.e. $f_c(\sigma = 0) = 1$. On the contrary, if a source is very inaccurate, or even independent of the reality observed (i.e. $\sigma \rightarrow +\infty$), it is incompetent, and its competence measure is such that $\lim\limits_{\sigma \rightarrow +\infty} f_c(\sigma) = 0$. Similarly, if we consider two information sources S_i and S_j of the same kind, which observe the same phenomenon, but with various levels of accuracy, i.e. $\sigma_i \neq \sigma_j$, f_c must satisfy the following property:

$$\forall i,j \in N, i \neq j, \ \sigma_i \leq \sigma_j \Rightarrow \text{Comp}_i \geq \text{Comp}_j. \hspace{2cm} [4.2]$$

The function f_c shown here depends on only one parameter but may be more or less complex. Our goal is to consider different functions. Considering the hypotheses recalled in section 4.4.2 and the relative accuracy levels of the positioning sensors – typically an average error of the order of 10^{-5} for a latitude measured by a GPS – it is suitable to choose the simple function $\frac{1}{1+\sigma}$ as a competence measurement [COS 17].

4.4.2.2. Measuring sincerity

It is inherently difficult to assess the sincerity of a source. It must be assessed based on the information sent by other sources [PAG 14]. It is important to highlight that competence and sincerity are intertwined. In fact, when a source is incompetent, it sends a highly inaccurate piece of information, which complicates its comparison with information provided by competent sources. The degree of imprecision of information corresponds to its distance from reality and, consequently, from other more precise information of the same kind. Therefore, when the competence of a source is poor, so will its sincerity. On the contrary, when a source is highly competent (i.e. a value close to 1), no conclusion about its sincerity can be drawn. Thus, our aim is to establish how the sincerity of a source can be measured through its competence:

$$\forall i \geq 1 \ \ \text{Sinc}_i(t) = \min(p_i(t), \text{Comp}_i(t)) \hspace{2cm} [4.3]$$

where $p_i \in [0; 1]$ represents the degree of agreement between the source i and the other sources at the instant t. The degree of agreement between a source and the other sources can be measured by comparing the information provided by the former with that sent by the other sources. It will be high if the information sent by the source agrees with that of the other sources.

Thus, if we consider a set of competent sources, a source that sends information similar to the majority will be judged to be more sincere than a disputed source (i.e. one that agrees with a minority). As it has been defined, the degree of agreement measures consensus and defines to which extent a source is supported by other sources. It may be regarded as the ratio between the number of sources in agreement with the source i at the instant t and the total number of sources. To measure the agreement between two sources, we propose, using a continuous similarity function called Sim so as to measure the correspondence by taking into consideration the information sent in the previous instants:

$$p_i(t) = 1 \qquad\qquad\qquad n = 1 \quad [4.4]$$

$$p_i(t) = \frac{1}{n-1}\sum_{\{j=1, j \neq 1\}}^{n} \; \text{Sim}\left(\{l_i(t)\}_{t>0}, \{l_j(t)\}_{t>0}\right) \quad n > 1 \quad [4.5]$$

where n is the number of sources and $\{l_i(t)\}_{t>0}$ is the set of information sent by the source i until the instant t. To ensure that $p_i = 1$ when all the sources are in agreement and, conversely, that $p_i = 0$ when the source i is opposed to all the other sources, the similarity function employed above implies measuring the correlation between the information provided by the different sources. Another advantage of this measurement is that the value of p_i is relatively stable when the number of sources n is "sufficiently" large. On the contrary, in the specific case of a single source, no consensus can be measured due to the lack of supplementary information. Thus, we conventionally set $p_1(t) = 1$, which illustrates that the source agrees with itself. This results in the direct equivalence between the sincerity of a single source and its competence (i.e. $\text{Sinc}_i(t) = \text{Comp}_i(t)$ for any t).

4.4.2.3. From competence and sincerity to trust

Liu and Williams [LIU 02] have proposed several solutions to measure a trust value $\text{Conf}(S_i)$ based on competence and sincerity measurements (i.e. $\text{Conf}(S_i) = \text{Conf}(\text{Comp}(S_i), \text{Sinc}(S_i))$. These measurements must satisfy all of the following constraints:

$$\text{Conf}(1,1) = 1 \qquad\qquad\qquad\qquad [4.6]$$

$$\text{Conf}(0,0) = 0 \qquad\qquad\qquad\qquad [4.7]$$

$$\text{Conf}(\text{Comp}, 1) = \text{Comp}, \text{Comp} \in [0; 1] \qquad [4.8]$$

$$\text{Conf}(1, \text{Sinc}) = \text{Sinc}, \text{Sinc} \in [0; 1]. \qquad [4.9]$$

Thus, several measures are suggested in keeping with these constraints:

$$\text{Conf}_1(\text{Comp}, \text{Sinc}) = \text{Comp} * \text{Sinc} \qquad [4.10]$$

$$\text{Conf}_2(\text{Comp}, \text{Sinc}) = \min(\text{Comp}, \text{Sinc}) \qquad \qquad [4.11]$$

$$\text{Conf}_3(\text{Comp}, \text{Sinc}) = 1 - (1 - \text{Comp})(1 - \text{Sinc}). \qquad \qquad [4.12]$$

The measure Conf_3 does not necessarily represent a lack of trust in an incompetent or insincere source. Specifically, Conf_3 is not equal to zero when the competence or sincerity of a source is equal to zero – a desirable property in our context. This means adding the following extra rules to the previous set of constraints:

$$\text{Conf}(0, \text{Sinc}) = 0, \text{Sinc} \in [0; 1] \qquad \qquad [4.13]$$

$$\text{Conf}(\text{Comp}, 0) = 0, \text{Comp} \in [0; 1]. \qquad \qquad [4.14]$$

Besides the various properties of the measures mentioned in this section, we should also consider the monotonicity of the measurements according to the variables on which they depend. For example, competence decreases in relation to the inaccuracy of a source: the more inaccurate a source is, the less competent it is. On the contrary, sincerity increases in relation to competence and consensus. Out of the two equally competent sources, the more sincere is the one in agreement with the majority. Conversely, if two sources are equally in agreement with the remaining sources, then the more competent one is regarded as more sincere. The same properties apply to trust measurements: out of two equally competent sources (with respect to sincerity), the one with more trust is the more sincere one (in relation to the more competent one).

4.5. Applying these notions to maritime geolocation data

The recent and widespread digitization of everyday life has affected the maritime field too. Currently, numerous data producers, measuring systems, and sensors produce various types of information about the state of the oceans, seafloors, and vessel or wildlife tracking. This information, which is essentially geographic, is measured, produced, collected, and exchanged by a high number of actors who interact simultaneously using various and highly heterogeneous mechanisms. In these conditions, it occasionally becomes difficult to establish the source of information, and even more so to ensure its integrity and to trust it. In fact, at each step of its life cycle, information faces a number of factors that threaten its integrity, questioning the trust that we may have in it. Navigation information related to maritime data has been increasingly collected, processed, analyzed, and displayed in conjunction with the generalization of collaborative positioning systems.

4.5.1. *The Automatic Identification System*

More specifically, the AIS (Automatic Identification System), used to track vessels at sea, is an interesting example that can be used to illustrate the integrity and trust issues of geolocated information. The AIS was established in 2000 by the International Maritime Organization (IMO) as part of the SOLAS (Safety of Life at Sea) convention "for all ships of 300 gross tonnage and upward engaged on international voyages, cargo ships of 500 gross tonnage and upward, and passenger ships, irrespective of size" [IMO 04]. This system, initially designed for collision avoidance, works using worldwide dedicated frequencies in the Marine VHF (Very High Frequency) band by sending messages to and receiving messages from surrounding stations (vessels or coastal stations), in a ca. 60 NM radius.

4.5.2. *Integrity and trust issues linked to the AIS*

In the last few years, AIS data have been used for maritime traffic control and surveillance purposes (e.g. risk analysis, interventions at sea) despite some problems inherent in the system. In fact, studies have revealed the vulnerability of this anti-collision system, which provides invaluable navigation assistance. The AIS is especially prone to errors and misuses [IPH 17b, RAY 15]. Thus, it has been affected by the transmission of false data (around 50% of the messages) [HAR 07], impersonation [MAR 12], vessel disappearance [WIN 14], and the transmission of false GPS coordinates (1% of the vessels broadcast falsified data), false statements about activities [KAT 14], and the creation of false vessel tracks or false alarms [BAL 14]. These errors and misuses create risks for the vessels themselves (grounding), other vessels (collisions), the environment (pollution), and for society (terrorism).

Besides, since the AIS system is not protected, it is particularly easy for an external person to hack it, as shown in the past by synthetic messages sent by non-existent vessels. Recently, several works have pointed out the shortcomings of this system and some possible degradations of the quality of the information sent by vessels mostly due to negligence and malice

[BAL 14, RAY 15]. Thus, possible errors, tampering, and breaches affecting the AIS have been listed.

In 2013, for demonstration purposes, [BHA 17] hacked into the onboard GPS in order to hijack a vessel by deceiving its automatic pilot and indicating that the vessel had veered off its initial course (unbeknownst to the crew who, however, were aware of the experiment), thus forcing it to adjust its course and change the route initially expected.

The issue that concerns the integrity of geographic data, and therefore trust, is illustrated below by situations that illustrate cases of inconsistency between two consecutive points. Figure 4.2 shows four typical scenarios (series of AIS positions) that are *a priori* abnormal and yet have been identified in the AIS dataflow.

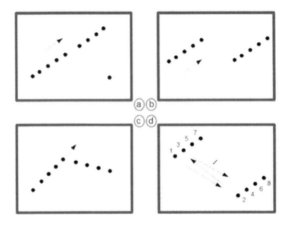

Figure 4.2. *Scenarios that present a kinematically inconsistent situation*

Situation (a) represents a simple irregular point that follows an apparently consistent trajectory, where each point represents a vessel position. This is typical for a GPS tracking system error (longitudinal offset, latitudinal offset, or both), but it may also be due to tampering. Case (b) shows the raw offset of a trajectory that seems normal before and after the offset. This type of behavior may be caused by a problem with the software or the equipment, or it may even be due to a case of external hacking. However, it is often caused by the crew's tampering. Case (c) illustrates a sharp change, of course, that is not compatible with the characteristics of the vessel or the destination information it claims to have. The causes are generally the same as in the previous case. Finally, case (d) shows the course of a vessel traveling between two places that are more or less distant, apparently creating two distinct courses followed by two vessels that sail with the same vessel identifier. This is typical in cases of impersonation or shared identities (e.g. port services).

4.5.3. *A suitable system for a range of analyses*

The information sent by the AIS, which may involve integrity and trust issues, is structured in 27 messages (position report, specific information, and control messages), which each contain 5–15 data fields. The transmission rate is contextual and varies in relation to the speed of the vessel: from 2 s, when the speed is more than 23 knots, to 3 min, when the vessel is not moving in case of position report messages.

Thus, the AIS presents a complex structure and behavior, which includes different messages, each of which is assigned to a specific use. Consequently, each message will contain data fields that are specific for a given use. For example, a message that contains dynamic information (e.g. number 1) will include, among other things, latitude, longitude, course over ground, and speed over ground (called "course" and "speed," respectively, in the rest of this chapter), whereas a message that contains static information (e.g. number 5) will send, among other things, destination information, the name of the vessel, as well as its dimensions. Some data fields are included in various types of messages, for example, those that contain information on the position of the transmitting station (longitude and latitude), which are included in 10 out of the 27 types of messages.

It is crucial to catalog in a specific manner each field of the system and to identify those that are similar in order to analyze the integrity of the AIS. To that end, an "XXY" classification has been established. Here, XX could be two numbers between 01 and 27 which represent the number of the message, whereas Y represents a letter that classes the fields in ascending order starting from A. Thus, a "04E" classification represents the fifth field of message number 4.

There are various kinds of AIS data. In fact, six types of fields can be listed in these messages. Thus, a field can include a numerical value that represents a physical quantity (e.g. speed), a choice out of a predefined list of values (e.g. a navigational status), an identifier (e.g. the MMSI – unique ship identifier), a textual value (e.g. the name of the vessel), a binary value, or a date value. The range of types of data fields, together with the wide variety of types of messages, makes it harder to analyze the data.

4.5.4. *A suitable system for assessing integrity*

The AIS is perfectly adapted to the four-step analysis of integrity described in section 4.3.2, since vessels send messages of various kinds, the pieces of information included in a message may coincide, and different messages contain identical or matching pieces of information. A list of integrity items has been established for each step of the analysis of the aforementioned data, totaling 935 indicators of integrity across the four steps [IPH 17a].

These indicators have been associated with complementary data sources so as to determine four types of alerts: alerts related to the indicators of integrity that result from the analysis of AIS messages, alerts related to the vessel, alerts related to the potential scenarios faced by a vessel, and alerts that describe the maritime situation. Ultimately, combining these alerts allows us to define the associated risks (e.g. illegal fishing, piracy, illegal immigration).

The variety of complementary contextual data is essential for a more thorough analysis of the integrity of an AIS message or series of messages. In fact, some data may exhibit an abnormal or forbidden behavior. For example, integrating marine protected areas (e.g. Natura 2000) allows us to chart the course of the ships that sail across them. Similarly, weather data may enable us to understand a trend that seemed abnormal at first glance or, on the contrary, to draw attention to a seemingly normal trend that becomes abnormal when the extra data available are taken into account. Several categories of contextual data may be used: environmental data (e.g. related to meteorology or bathymetry), data on the vessel (such as the examination of vessel registers), or data related to maritime navigation (marine areas, maritime routes, and origin/destination matrices).

Indicators and alerts have been formalized through algorithms, thanks to description logics, so as to obtain a rigorous representation that makes it easier to understand them and to consider how they can be exploited and developed [IPH 17a]. This formalism or description language allows us to model the bodies of knowledge manipulated through terminological axioms

(TBox), which describe general knowledge (concepts and roles), and assertional axioms (ABox), which describe a specific state of the body of knowledge in which individuals are identified. Resorting to a formalization based on description logics makes it possible to assess the integrity of the value of data fields logically and systematically. Indicators, which are deterministic due to the use of this description logic, provide as an output a Boolean result, displaying the value FALSE if no integrity problem arises, and the value TRUE if the data analysis highlights a fault in the integrity of the data. Below, we provide an example of an indicator and an example of an alert formalized through description logics.

EXAMPLE 4.1.– *The indicator 16M01 which verifies the fields C (the sender's MMSI number) and E (the receiver's MMSI number) in message 16.*

The goal of this indicator is to verify whether the MMSI number (Maritime Mobile Service Identity) of the source of message m, sent at time t and including data D, differs from that of the ship sending the message. This algorithm processes all the messages m of type 16 (M_{16}) in the interval studied T_c. The result is stored in R_m^{16M01}:

$$\forall m(D, t) \in M_{16}, D = \{id, sourcemmsi, destinationmmsi\}, t \in T_c \quad [4.15]$$

$$((sourcemmsi = destinationmmsi) \vdash R_m^{16M01} \leftarrow \top) \quad [4.16]$$

$$(\neg(sourcemmsi = destinationmmsi) \vdash R_m^{16M01} \leftarrow \bot) \quad [4.17]$$

EXAMPLE 4.2.– The alert f_isInTSS, which verifies whether a ship that sends a message m, at time t and including data D, is part of a Traffic Separation Scheme (TSS) whose spatial extension is A. This algorithm processes all the messages m of type 1 (M_1) in the interval studied T_c. The result is stored in $f_{isInTSS}$.

$$\forall m(D, t) \in M_1, D = \{id, lon, lat\}, t \in T_c \quad [4.18]$$

$$(((lon, lat) \in A) \vdash (f_{isInTSS} \leftarrow \top)) \quad [4.19]$$

$$((\neg((lon, lat) \in A)) \vdash (f_{isInTSS} \leftarrow \bot)) \quad [4.20]$$

Several scenarios have been contrived to test indicators and alerts and to individually assess how these numerous algorithms work, especially for the detection of kinematic inconsistencies. The following illustrations

(Figures 4.3 and 4.4) provide the examples of two scenarios (Figure 4.2, cases (a) and (c) built with a set of nine points). The first case, presented in Figure 4.3, represents a trajectory in which a point is off the expected course. The kinematic data about all the other points are consistent, especially speed, course, and the distance between points. The fifth point presents a difference of 0.02 degrees southward of its expected position.

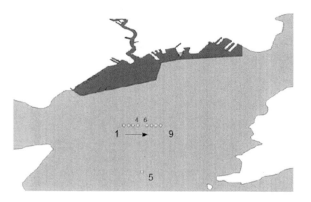

Figure 4.3. *An integrity scenario showing a case of position inconsistency. For a color version of this figure, see www.iste.co.uk/batton/geographic1.zip*

Table 4.1 presents the results of the alerts sent out. The alert *f_suddenapp* is sent out if a vessel appears for the first time in an area where no vessel is expected to appear; the alert *f_nextposition* indicates that the position of a vessel does not correspond to its position and kinematic values; finally, the alert *f_ubiquity* is sent out when the positions of a vessel vary too much in a short period of time. The next position and ubiquity alerts were sent out for points 5 and 6. It should be pointed out that the ubiquity alert was sent out because the points are distant enough.

	1	2	3	4	5	6	7	8	9
f_suddenapp	☐								
f_nextposition					✓	✓			
f_ubiquity					✓	✓			

Table 4.1. *Position piracy alerts*

In the second case, presented in Figure 4.4, the course presented is at first northward as far as point 5, then due east. However, the kinematic data transmitted (course and route) indicate that the course is still northward, which results in the triggering of an alert of inconsistent successive points, specifically points 6–9.

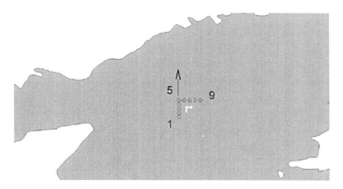

Figure 4.4. *An integrity scenario showing kinematic information inconsistency. For a color version of this figure, see www.iste.co.uk/batton/geographic1.zip*

Table 4.2 sums up the alerts that were sent out in this scenario. The ubiquity alert was never sent out because each point is situated within the radius accessible from the previous point.

	1	2	3	4	5	6	7	8	9
f_suddenapp	☐								
f_nextposition						☐	☐	☐	☐

Table 4.2. *Alerts sent out because of dynamic data inconsistency*

Thus, these alerts, associated with contextual information (e.g. weather, oceanographic, or statutory data), allow us to assess the associated maritime risks (e.g. illegal fishing or terrorism). Three dimensions should be prioritized when assessing risks: the human aspect linked to the safety of human life at sea, the environmental aspect related to the protection of the environment, and the infrastructural aspect linked to the possible damage caused to ports and the structure of ships. This assessment can, in its simplest form, be made by associating the alerts deterministically while also considering risks in relation to their type (collision, grounding, piracy or terrorism, illegal fishing, and smuggling of goods or individuals) and level (low, moderate, high, and very high). These two aspects are established, thanks to the knowledge imparted by experts in the maritime sector. This information is later used by monitoring centers that will interpret the situation and plan an intervention in the field.

4.5.5. *A suitable system for measuring trust*

The scenarios in which experiments on trust have been carried out are built on the basis of original data obtained by the AIS. These data are about a cargo vessel, which was chosen for its stable speed (thus, a vessel traveling at a constant speed sends messages at regular intervals, in keeping with the model we introduced in section 4.4.2.1).

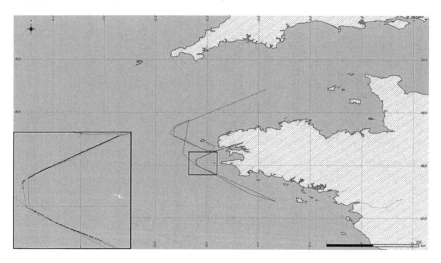

Figure 4.5. *Course and position of the ship studied. For a color version of this figure, see www.iste.co.uk/batton/geographic1.zip*

Figure 4.5 shows the navigation data on the container vessel on the night between March 21 and 22, 2015, off the coast of Brest (France). The information available includes heading, speed, geographic coordinates (latitude and longitude), time, rate of turn, and the course of the vessel.

Based on these data, we have simulated three information sources: two GPSs and a Doppler log, each of which provides information about speed.

These sources of information can be found aboard ships like cruise vessels. In our experimental context, the two GPSs are situated at the bow and at the stern of the vessel, respectively, and the Doppler log is located in the middle. If a GPS can send several types of information (position, course, and speed), a Doppler log sends only one piece of information, i.e. speed. In fact, a Doppler log measures the speed of a ship in relation to the seabed by using an ultrasonic signal. The requirements for the experiment led us to choose only three sources. In order to be measured, sincerity needs redundancy, namely, the availability of several sources that send the same piece of information. However, in practice, vessels often cannot rely on many sensors that send the same information. Vessels of a certain size (such as cruising vessels) can do this more often.

Thus, simulating three sources is a good compromise which provides a realistic number of sensors and makes it possible to test the measurements established in this chapter by exploiting the redundancy of the information. To simulate the three sources, a normally distributed Gaussian noise was added by following the source model described in section 4.4.2.1. The three Gaussian noises have equal variance, which was drawn from the manufacturers' specifications. The noise of a source $i \in \{1, 2, 3\}$ has variance $\sigma_i = 0,1$, yielding a competence measurement:

$$\text{Comp}_i(t) = \frac{1}{1+\sigma_i} \approx 0,91. \qquad [4.21]$$

In our scenario, the goal is to simulate an attack on one of the sensors. In fact, a hacker may want to send false information about speed to slow down a vessel (e.g. to make it easier for pirates to intercept it) or to make it go faster (e.g. to cause fuel overconsumption or the accelerated wear of the engine or of the driveshaft). This attack, even if quite blatant (it would be enough to look at the history to detect it), may turn out to be inconvenient and even dangerous in the long term. We have extracted a stream of 1,000 pieces of data on speed from the 9,639 pieces of data provided by the AIS (Figure 4.5), added noise to the information to simulate the sources, and taken various measurements described in the previous sections. Before adding noise, the information about speed is modified. This simulates how a hacker tampers with the information destined to the Doppler log. The fact that the information is altered before the addition of noise is typical of a spoofing attack.

Figure 4.6 shows the trends of various competence, sincerity, and trust measurements by simulating the three sources of speed based on the data produced by the AIS. To simulate a spoofing attack, the Doppler log sends false information starting from the moment $t = 500$. From then on, the speed sent is one knot greater than the actual speed.

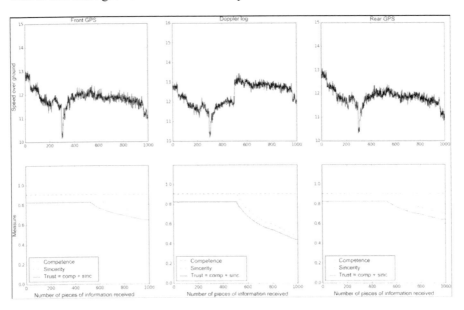

Figure 4.6. *Changes in the competence, sincerity, and trust measurements when there are three sources of speed on a ship. For a color version of this figure, see www.iste.co.uk/batton/geographic1.zip*

The first curves in Figure 4.6 show the speed perceived by each source with a precision of around 0.1 knots (the manufacturer's specifications). The Competence, Sincerity, and Trust curves show, respectively, for each source, how competence, sincerity, and trust change over time. Trust is measured here as the product of the two previous measurements. In particular, the *Sincerity* curve highlights the tampered information sent by the Doppler log. As shown in Figure 4.6, the competence of each source is the same, because noise of the same variance has been added to the actual data. We can observe the impact of the Doppler log attack on the sincerity measurements for the three sources. As the log indicates a different speed from that measured by the GPSs, its measured sincerity declines, and more significantly than the sincerity of the two GPSs.

The results observed in several scenarios and by considering various distances reveal that analyzing quality through the lens of trust is a relevant measurement, especially for geographic information. The functions tested respond well to data altered on purpose: the trust measured is lower when a source is attacked. Therefore, this type of measurement can detect changes in information. On the other hand, the decrease of trust is proportional to the strength of the attack. This also applies to the logic that guides a detection process: the less a hacker attempts to hide, the easier it becomes to observe their maneuvers.

4.6. Conclusion

An essential element, which is recent and simultaneously still in the middle of a revolution and in a state of flux, is substantially changing the way in which research must grasp the notions and problems linked to the quality of geographic information: the emergence of individualized positioning systems that can track people, means of transport, and other digital (online) objects. These various systems generate a multitude of location data that are by now shared live, either directly among users or on social networks.

While digitization presents numerous advantages, it also creates numerous shortcomings, which are significantly accentuated by a mass effect, in the control of internal and external quality. In this context, the integrity and trust measurements mentioned in this chapter represent methods that are necessary to detect shortcomings – if not to discover more of them – in the data quality required. The issues that concern this field are becoming more significant and require research to explore new avenues, so as to establish the risks (and consequences) involved in decision-support processes and related to the vulnerability and misuse of the data and information manipulated and/or exchanged.

We know that high volumes of data produced at present are copied and disseminated very quickly to a large number of users. Therefore, the dissemination of data cannot be controlled by the data producer. If, as we have seen in this chapter, it remains difficult to assess the internal and external quality of a piece of information, communicating the data/quality combination related to a given use is even harder. In fact, most data quality assessments are not communicated. Furthermore, if a user tells other users that a dataset is of good quality, nothing guarantees that these users will employ the same dataset without making any changes. The software is updated when security holes have been discovered. Likewise, once it has been discovered that some data have been altered, the fact should be communicated to all its users. It is crucial to trace data and their assessment in order to minimize the risk of using data such as that produced by collaborative networks, which turn out to be very vulnerable to tampering.

4.7. References

[AGU 98] AGUMYA A., HUNTER G.J., "Fitness for use: reducing the impact of geographic information uncertainty", in *Proceedings of URISA 98 Conference*, Charlotte, NC, USA, pp. 245–254, July 18–22, 1998.

[BAL 14] BALDUZZI M., PASTA A., WILHOIT K., "A security evaluation of AIS automated identification system", in *Proceedings of the 30th Annual Computer Security Applications Conference, ACSAC'14*, ACM, New Orleans, LA, USA, pp. 436–445, 2014.

[BHA 17] BHATTI J., HUMPHREYS T.E., "Hostile control of ships via false GPS signals demonstration and detection", *Journal of the Institute of Navigation*, vol. 34, no. 1, pp. 51–66, 2017.

[BLO 97] BLOMQVIST K., "The many faces of trust", *Scandinavian Journal of Management*, vol. 13, no. 3, pp. 271–286, 1997.

[CER 10] CERTU, La qualité des données géographiques : état des lieux pour un débat, Report, Centre d'études sur les réseaux, les transports, l'urbanisme et les constructions publiques, Lyon, France, 2010.

[CHA 09] CHANDOLA V., BANERJEE A., KUMAR V., "Anomaly detection: a survey", *ACM Computing Surveys*, vol. 41, no. 3, pp. 1–58, 2009.

[COS 16] COSTE B., RAY C., COATRIEUX G., "Évaluation de la confiance dans un environnement multisources", in *Atelier sécurité des systèmes d'information : technologies et personnes, informatique des organisations et systèmes d'information et de décision (INFORSID)*, Grenoble, France, 2016.

[COS 17] COSTE B., RAY C., COATRIEUX G., "Modèle et mesures de confiance pour la sécurité des systèmes d'information", *Ingénierie des Systèmes d'Information*, vol. 22, no. 2/17, pp. 19–41, 2017.

[DEM 01] DEMOLOMBE R., "To trust information sources: a proposal for a modal logical framework", in *Trust and Deception in Virtual Societies*, Kluwer, Dordrecht, The Netherlands, pp. 111–124, 2001.

[DEU 58] DEUTSCH M., "Trust and suspicion", *Journal of Conflict Resolution*, vol. 2, no. 4, pp. 265–279, 1958.

[FIS 01] FISHER C.W., KINGMA B.R., "Criticality of data quality as exemplified in two disasters", *Information and Management*, vol. 39, no. 2, pp. 109–116, 2001.

[GER 03] GERVAIS M., Pertinence d'un manuel d'instructions au sein d'une stratégie de gestion du risque juridique découlant de la fourniture de données géographiques numériques, PhD thesis, Université de Marne-la-Vallée, France, 2003.

[GRA 00] GRANDISON T., SLOMAN M., "A survey of trust in internet applications", *IEEE Communications Surveys & Tutorials*, vol. 3, no. 4, pp. 2–16, 2000.

[HAR 01] HARTMANN S., BOVENS L., "A probabilistic theory of the coherence of an information set", in BECKERMANN A. (ed.), *Argument & Analysis: Proceedings of the 4th International Congress of the Society for Analytical Philosophy*, Ansgar Beckermann Ed., Bielefeld, Germany, pp. 195–206, 2001.

[HAR 07] HARATI-MOKHTARI A., WALL A., BROOKS P. *et al.*, "Automatic identification system (AIS): a human factors approach", *Journal of Navigation*, vol. 60, no. 3, pp. 373–389, 2007.

[IMO 04] IMO, *International Convention for the Safety of Life at Sea (SOLAS)*, International treaty, International Maritime Organisation, London, UK, 2004.

[IPH 17a] IPHAR C., Formalisation of a data analysis environment based on anomaly detection for risk assessment – application to maritime domain awareness, PhD thesis, MINES ParisTech, PSL Research University, France, 2017.

[IPH 17b] IPHAR C., NAPOLI A., RAY C., "Integrity assessment of a worldwide maritime tracking system for a geospatial analysis at sea", in *Proceedings of the 20th International Conference on Geographic Information Science (AGILE)*, May 2017, Wageningen, The Netherlands, 2017.

[JOU 14] JOUSSELME A.-L., BOURY-BRISSET A.-C., DEBAQUE B. *et al.*, "Characterization of hard and soft sources of information: a practical illustration", in *17th International Conference on Information Fusion*, Salamanca, Spain, pp. 1–8, 2014.

[KAT 14] KATSILIERIS F., BRACA P., CORALUPPI S., "Detection of malicious AIS position spoofing by exploiting radar information", in *16th International Conference on Information Fusion*, Istanbul, Turkey, pp. 1196–1203, 2014.

[LAX 11] LAXHAMMAR R., Anomaly detection in trajectory data for surveillance applications, PhD thesis, School of Science and Technology, Örebro University, Örebro, Sweden, 2011.

[LEW 85] LEWIS J.D., WEIGERT A., "Trust as a social reality", *Social Forces*, vol. 63, no. 4, pp. 967–985, 1985.

[LIU 02] LIU W., WILLIAMS M.-A., "Trustworthiness of information sources and information pedigrees", *Intelligent Agents VIII*, Springer, Berlin, Germany, pp. 290–306, 2002.

[LOR 08] LORINI E., DEMOLOMBE R., "From binary trust to graded trust in information sources: a logical perspective", in FALCONE R., BARBER S.K., SABATER-MIR J. *et al.* (eds), *Trust in Agent Societies, TRUST 2008*, Lecture Notes in Computer Science, vol. 5396, Springer, Berlin, Germany, 2008.

[LUH 79] LUHMANN N., *Trust and Power*, U.M.I., John Wiley and Sons, New York, USA, 1979.

[MAR 94] MARSH S.P., Formalising trust as a computational concept, PhD thesis, Department of Computer Science and Mathematics, University of Stirling, Stirling, UK, 1994.

[MAR 12] MARITIME EXECUTIVE, "Iran, Tanzania and falsifying AIS signals to trade with Syria", available at: https://www.maritime-executive.com/article/iran-tanzania-and-falsifying-ais-signals-to-trade-with-syria, 12 December 2012.

[MCK 00] MCKNIGHT D.H., CHERVANY N.L., "What is trust? A conceptual analysis and an interdisciplinary model", in *Americas Conference on Information Systems (AMCIS)*, Long Beach, CA, USA, pp. 827–833, 2000.

[PAG 14] PAGLIERI F., CASTELFRANCHI C., DA COSTA PEREIRA C. *et al.*, "Trusting the messenger because of the message: feedback dynamics from information quality to source evaluation", *Computational and Mathematical Organization Theory*, vol. 20, no. 2, pp. 176–194, 2014.

[PIE 10] PIERKOT C., "Vers un usage éclairé de la donnée géographique", in *Proceedings of the 10th Conférence Internationale Francophone sur l'Extraction et la Gestion de Connaissances (EGC)*, Revue des Nouvelles Technologies de l'Information, Hammamet, Tunisia, 2010.

[PIE 11] PIERKOT C., ZIMANYI E., LIN Y. *et al.*, "Advocacy for external quality in GIS", in *Proceedings of the 4th International Conference on GeoSpatial Semantics, GeoS'11*, Springer-Verlag, Brest, France, pp. 151–165, 2011.

[RAY 15] RAY C., IPHAR C., NAPOLI A. *et al.*, "DeAIS project: detection of AIS spoofing and resulting risks", *OCEANS'15 MTS/IEEE*, Genoa, Italy, May 2015.

[WAN 95] WANG R.Y., REDDY M.P., KON H.B., "Toward quality data: an attribute-based approach", *Decision Support Systems*, vol. 13, nos 3–4, pp. 349–372, 1995.

[WAN 96] WANG R.Y., STRONG D.M., "Beyond accuracy: what data quality means to data consumers", *Journal of Management Information Systems*, vol. 12, no. 4, pp. 5–33, 1996.

[WAN 10] WANG T., BEBBINGTON M., HARTE D., "A comparative study of coherence, mutual information and cross-intensity models", *International Journal of Information and Systems Sciences*, vol. 6, no. 1, pp. 49–60, 2010.

[WIN 14] WINDWARD, AIS data on the high seas: an analysis of the magnitude and implications of growing data manipulation at sea, Report, Winward Company, Tel Aviv, Israel, 2014.

Part 2

Representation

Formalisms and Representations of Imperfect Geographic Objects

5.1. Theories about the representation of an imperfect geographic object

Chapter 3 introduces the construction of spatial data and the identification of its related spatial object, i.e. the so-called generation phase. These stages make it possible to distinguish between two types of imperfections: the imperfection caused by the simplification of the real world when data are produced and the imperfections that emerge during the acquisition and creation of a geographic database. These kinds of imperfections are fundamentally different. The former type of imperfection involves the choice and hypotheses related to the outline adopted. In fact, any spatial representation model is conditioned and only applies to the hypotheses made (the choice of spatial model, accuracy, representation) for a given use[1]. In this case, the absence of a specification or representation of the object does not constitute an error but an omission or a lack of knowledge. On the other hand, when a spatial object can be identified or is identifiable, its imperfection is linked to the structuring process, which may generate errors and uncertainties through the manipulation of these objects.

Even if *a priori* omission and lack of knowledge are often associated with the conceptual phase of an outline (or model), while imprecision and

---

Chapter written by Mireille BATTON-HUBERT and François PINET.

1 EXAMPLE.– A road network map is drawn for a specific use (to calculate travel times) with a given vector model, on a specific scale, and with a certain degree of accuracy, but it is not necessarily appropriate if the aim is to calculate potential aquaplaning effects on the road.

uncertainty are linked to the stage during which information is manipulated, the same mathematical formalisms will often be used in both cases. In fact, this book endeavors to formalize imperfection and ways of processing imperfect spatial and geographic data. Thus, the concepts and types of uncertainty manipulated will be grasped without referring beforehand to the origin of this uncertainty and its correction.

The issue is to define an imperfect spatial object based on theories of uncertainty and the awareness of this attribute in the formalisms of the geographic object. This way of developing a geographic spatial object simultaneously requires the development of the related data schema and the topology of objects in space and time. Built on the basis of algebra and the algebra of relations, topological relationships are re-established for these new imperfect objects. In this chapter, some of these aspects will be tackled through examples that introduce the tools and elements presented in the following chapters.

After showing some examples of geographic data and spatial information to illustrate where and how imperfection takes shape, this chapter aims to provide the mathematical tools for the main theories used to manipulate the imperfection that affects a geographic object.

5.2. Where and when do we refer to imperfection in geographic information?

This section employs some examples to present *on which basis* and *how* it is possible to introduce the notion of the imperfection of a spatial and geographic object:

EXAMPLE 5.1.– Let us imagine the following context: after an earthquake, the emergency services want to find out whether one of the bridges in the area hit by the earthquake is still functional. Let us not try to find an answer. On the contrary, let us analyze the available information. The geographic object in question is a bridge in terms of structure, characterized by the following attribute: "allowing vehicles to cross". Before the earthquake, its attribute was "being geolocated". The bridge was entered as a vector point object into a GIS database.

We are interested in finding out whether this bridge can be crossed. Several situations emerge:

– the bridge exists or no longer exists, but no one has been able to see it: there is a complete lack of knowledge about both the fact "the bridge exists" and the fact "the bridge no longer exists";

– the bridge may still exist, but no one is sure: there is a partial lack of knowledge.

– a bridge exists, but its exact position is unknown: there is imprecision about the location, and, therefore, the information is vague.

– the condition of the bridge may be completely ignored or partially assessed. In that case, some confidence is granted to the fact that *the bridge is functional or not.*

In this example, the fact will allow us to distinguish whether "*the bridge exists*" is a possibility or not. Confidence is associated with a value related to this fact, and it will be assigned to it, for example, depending on the ability of the bridge to withstand shocks. Uncertainty concerns various precise values related to this fact and the agreement between this information and reality. On the contrary, the attribute of the bridge that characterizes it as a "*functional bridge*" depends on the level of damage qualitatively perceived and described ("certainly" or "*a priori*" *functional*) by an observer. Imprecision does not determine the outline of values assigned by the attribute of the object.

Finally, the knowledge about the functional state of a bridge may be imprecise and uncertain when the state of knowledge is: "the bridge may be functional to a degree that corresponds to slightly more than half its bearing capacity".

EXAMPLE 5.2.– In the context of water resources, a decision-maker is often led to estimate the resource available in a given point of the geographic space: they can rely on measuring points for water level and natural outlet flows. Their goal is to assess the most productive points, but the information available is limited as there are only a few drilling measurements. The decision-maker is aware that the resource exists, but they do not know if it will be enough to meet the demand. Let us analyze the information available. The geographic object used for an aquifer is a piezometric field, for which the value of a physical quantity is included in an attribute of the associated geometric object (continuous raster model or vector model with Euclidean geometry). This object may be geolocated, and it conforms a specific reality. The issue is to find out how much water can be produced by a specific point.

The objective is to discover the quantity produced by a well [situated in a point (x,y) of the geographic space]. We should point out several elements:

– Since the point is known, the quantity of water produced is unknown. An expert estimates it to be significantly greater than 5 m³/h. The lack of knowledge concerns the content of the information. Thus, the value of the attribute of the object is vague or fuzzy.

– Another expert estimates it to be greater than 5 m³/h. Their estimate is accurate and pinpoints a value (precise information; thus, we will say that the fact is sure). However, if the expert reconsiders their assessment, they may think that the estimate represents a possibility. Thus, they will assign certain reliability to this fact by qualifying it in terms of confidence. The information becomes uncertain. Similarly, a probabilistic estimator can calculate a value and a confidence interval by inference or interpolation. The values will be identified with the degree of reliability of their estimate; thus, we will refer to uncertainty.

EXAMPLE 5.3.– Let us present one last example which will be reconsidered in depth later on: a parcel of land may be classically seen as a polygon, i.e. a spatial object with specific attributes associated with it. Image classification is used to build land-cover plots based on continuous measurement data on wavelengths detected by satellite. Depending on the attribute examined, the boundary between the two areas cannot necessarily be identified through image processing. There may be some confusion according to the types of response. In this case, the boundary of a parcel is vague and delimited by two possible boundaries since the level of discrimination is low. In other cases, a plot belongs to a progressive type of land-cover. The former case refers to the imprecision that affects the content of the information, the latter refers to the membership of an event to a state.

In the last example, the spatial object becomes a fuzzy object whose definition becomes vague. It exists, but its geometry at least is imprecise.

These three examples present the way in which imprecision may be introduced and related to the information about a spatial geographic object. Each spatial geographic object becomes an imperfect spatial object whose geometric and topological model must be developed.

The following paragraphs provide the main mathematical tools used to formalize and manipulate those two concepts, namely, imperfection meant as partial knowledge and uncertainty meant as the correspondence and the difference between reality and an imperfect spatial geographic object. They will also reveal how incompleteness and inadequacy of information interact with uncertainty.

5.3. Formalisms

This part presents the main mathematical tools used to manipulate those two concepts, i.e. imperfection meant as partial knowledge and uncertainty meant as correspondence to reality, besides introducing the ways in which a geometric and topological object evolves. Finally, this section will present some methods, particularly in relation to usable capacities and conditioning.

5.3.1. *The notion of event*

We adopt the following definitions, which will allow us to introduce the main mathematical formalisms presented:

DEFINITION.– *A piece of information is uncertain for an agent if the agent does not know whether it is true.*

A piece of information is uncertain if its truthfulness is questioned (the reliability of a source) or if it involves a phenomenon that has not taken place yet and is inherently subject to variation (e.g. the result of a dice roll before playing).

DEFINITION.– *A piece of information is imprecise if it does not allow an agent to answer the question they are asking.*

[BOU 09] and [PAR 01] distinguish in detail between the various kinds of a pieces of information. We will only establish a state of knowledge, called epistemic state, as a body of generic knowledge, observations, or beliefs about the object studied.

Studying an evolving phenomenon requires knowledge of the set Ω of all the possible values of the attribute of an object, which are called possible states (or results). This set may or may not be countable. An event is the result of one or more results [DUB 88].

To formalize mathematically this state of knowledge, we consider Ω the set of possible states in the world. Every part A of Ω is an event, interpreted as the proposition "ω *belongs to A*", namely, $\ll \omega \in A \gg$.

Thus, the imprecision of a piece of information may result from the lack of information (e.g. knowledge of only the possible values – the support – of a random variable) and errors in systematic measurement or in an expert opinion (estimating the value of a parameter). An imprecise piece of information may be formalized as the event data $A \subseteq \Omega$, a disjunctive set which is not reduced to a singleton.

DEFINITION.– *Set and fuzzy set.*

As a subset X of Ω, the reference space is defined by a characteristic function μ_x such that:

$$\mu_X = \begin{cases} 1 \ if \ x \ \in X \\ 0 \ if \ x \ \notin X \end{cases}$$

The function μ_x is a binary function that specifies the (binary) way in which each element of Ω belongs to X. This type of reference set characterizes a classical set.

A fuzzy subset A of Ω is defined by its characteristic function μ_A of Ω in [0,1]. $\mu_A(x)$ for any $x \in \Omega$ is interpreted as the degree of membership of x to the fuzzy subset A. μ_A is the membership function for this set. A fuzzy set may be defined by:

$$\{(x, \mu_A(x)), x \in A \}.$$

The support of a fuzzy number is the set of points with a strictly positive membership $\mu_A(x) > 0$:

$$\mathrm{Supp}(\mu_A) = \{x \in \Omega, \mu_A(x) > 0\}.$$

The core of a fuzzy number is the set of points that belong completely to A:

$$\mathrm{Core}(\mu_A) = \{x \in \Omega, \mu_A(x) = 1 \}.$$

DEFINITION.– *Fuzzy set and stack of crisp sets, α-cuts.*

The α-cut of a fuzzy set μ_A is the binary set defined by:

$$\mu_\alpha = \{x \in \Omega, \mu_A(x) \geq \alpha\}.$$

A fuzzy set may be seen as a stack of α-cuts, which may be rebuilt based on them as follows:

$$\mu(x) = \int_0^1 \mu_\alpha(x)d\alpha = \quad \sup \min_{\alpha \in]0,1]}(\alpha, \mu_\alpha(x)).$$

There are ways of measuring fuzzy sets such as fuzzy cardinals, the cardinal of the support of μ, and also fuzzy measures such as the Hamming distance, the distance from the complement, or the distance from the closest binary set.

However, let us reconsider the three introductory examples, where we can identify to which type of reference set an attribute of an object or an object belongs.

– If we consider the example of the bridge, the elements of Ω {exists, does not exist} are in the classical case. If we introduce the imprecision dimension, we could obtain a complementary state {exists, does not exist, undefined}.

– If we consider the second example, the elements of Ω are the set of possible water level values in a given point (the space over which this value is defined, over $\mathbb{R}$).

– In image processing, Ω will constitute the definition space for the image (pixels) or the objects extracted from the image as polygons of the segments. A gray scale gradient in an image is the set of values assigned to the image for each pixel: the x value belongs to the reference space.

– A fuzzy set visualization becomes for each pixel a standardized value between [0,1], which corresponds to the degree of membership of the pixel to a ω category: if this value is equal to 0, it does not belong to this category; if it is equal to 1, it belongs to this category; otherwise it belongs to the fuzzy set A with the value $\mu_A(\omega)$: the universe is the set of possible ω categories.

A fuzzy number is a particular instance of a fuzzy set. It is normal, it has a unique core (there is only one x for which $\mu_A(x) = 1$), and it is convex and continuous. Therefore, it constitutes a fuzzy upper semi-continuous (u.s.c) interval with a compact and unimodal support[2].

The example in Figure 5.1 shows a fuzzy number used to represent the value equal to "around 5".

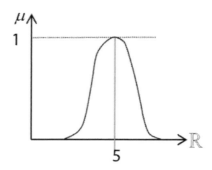

Figure 5.1. *A fuzzy number*

5.3.2. *Confidence and certainty (pre-measure and confidence measure)*

The uncertainty of a piece of information is, therefore, expressed by terms such as "probable", "possible", and "necessary", and it refers to the confidence between the association (object, attribute, value) in relation to a reality. Thus, it is associated either with the truthfulness of an event or with the result of a phenomenon which has not taken place yet and is subject to natural variability or randomness.

A frame of reference is a family T of parts of Ω called tribe that verifies the existence of an empty set, the complementary event, and the sequence of events: it is a σ-algebra, namely a stable family passing to complements, unions, and countable intersections.

The gradation of these qualifiers, i.e. *probable, possible,* and *necessary,* requires the introduction of functions used to quantify these event qualifiers.

We assign to the proposition $\omega \in A$ a belief indicator, which is numerical (for example, a probability) or linguistic ("it is possible/certain that").

2 A compact support is defined over a delimited closed interval like [a,b], and a fuzzy number only has one mode over this interval (only one "peak").

Mathematically, we usually choose to assign to each event A a number $g(A) \in [0,1]$ that measures the confidence of an agent in the proposition $\omega \in A$ called confidence pre-measure, so that a certain event is equal to 1 and an impossible event is equal to 0. It is obvious that any event will range between 0 and 1.

DEFINITION.– *Confidence measure.*

We define an application $g: \mathcal{P}(\Omega) \to [0,1]$, called confidence measure, such that:

$$g(\emptyset) = 0 , g(\Omega) = 1,$$

$$\forall A, B \in \mathcal{P}(\Omega), A \subseteq B \Rightarrow g(A) \leq g(B).$$

Thus, according to the monotonicity axiom, if the event A implies B, we have always as much confidence in B as we do in A. When the frame of reference is infinite, the continuity axioms may be introduced. They are not necessary for the construction of the confidence pre-measure because some confidence measures do not verify them (like possibilities). The confidence space is given by (Ω, T, g).

We refer to confidence pre-measures as the additive axiom for two separate events is not explicitly formulated [DUB 88].

These pre-measures may also be seen as the fuzzy measure of a crisp set [BLO 04] if the monotonicity and continuity axioms are respected. Among the families of fuzzy measures, we will focus on:

– probability measures (whose fuzzy λ-measures are obtained by relaxing the additivity constraint of the probability measures);

– belief and plausibility functions in the theory of belief functions;

– possibility measures.

DEFINITION.– *Probability.*

Any probability measure $\mathbb{P}$ on a measurable space is a self-dual confidence measure $(\mathbb{P}(A) = 1 - \mathbb{P}(\overline{A}))$, which in addition satisfies the σ-additivity property:

$$A \cap B = \emptyset \Rightarrow \mathbb{P}(A \cup B) = \mathbb{P}(A) + \mathbb{P}(B).$$

DEFINITION.– *Possibility and necessity measures.*

Any possibility measure is a fuzzy measure (in the finite case). It is a function of Π of $\mathcal{C}$ [3] in $[0,1]$ such that:

1. $\Pi(\emptyset) = 0$

2. $\Pi(\Omega) = 1$

3. $\forall\, I \subset \mathbb{N}, \forall\, A_i \sqsubseteq \Omega (i \in I), \Pi\left(\bigcup_{i\,\in I} A_i\right) = sup_{(i\in I)}\,\Pi(A_i).$

By duality, the necessary measure is defined as a function N of $\mathcal{C}$ in $[0,1]$ so that:

$$\forall A \subseteq \Omega, N(A) = 1 - \Pi(A^C)$$

verifying properties 1 and 2 as well as the following:

$$\forall\, I \subset \mathbb{N}, \forall\, A_i \sqsubseteq \Omega (i \in I), N\left(\bigcap_{i\,\in I} A_i\right) = inf_{(i\in I)}\,N(A_i).$$

If an event is necessary $(N(A) = 1)$, its opposite is impossible. Necessity measures the certainty of an event; the stronger it is, the less weak uncertainty is. Total ignorance is expressed by a necessity equal to zero.

DEFINITION.– *The mass function defined by Shafer* (1976) [SHA 76].

A mass function for a source of information (or evidence/proof) called Basic Belief Assignment (BBA) is a fuzzy measure $m^\Theta(.): 2^\Theta \rightarrow [0,1]$, such that:

$$m^\Theta(\emptyset) = 0$$

and

$$\sum_{A \subseteq \Theta} m^\Theta(A) = 1, \forall\, A \neq \emptyset \in 2^\Theta$$

where Θ, the Frame of Discernment (FoD), is a finite set of discrete elements $\Theta = \{\theta_1, \ldots, \theta_e, \ldots, \theta_n\}$ (with $n > 1$), whose elements are

---

3 $\mathcal{C}$: the set of crisp sets of Ω.

assumed to be exhaustive and mutually exclusive. The set 2^Θ, called "power-set of Θ", groups the singletons of Θ together with the subsets obtained through their unions and the singletons of the empty set.

Thus, for $n = 2$, we obtain $\Theta = \{\theta_1, \theta_2\}$ and $2^\Theta = \{\phi, \theta_1, \theta_2, \theta_1 \cup \theta_2\}$ with a mass function defined by:

$$m^\Theta(\emptyset) = 0 \text{ and } m^\Theta(\theta_1) + m^\Theta(\theta_2) + m^\Theta(\theta_1 \cup \theta_2) = 1.$$

Total ignorance about the frame of discernment requires all the masses of the elements of 2^Θ to be equal to zero, since only the union of all the hypotheses is equal to 1, namely, $m(\theta) = 1$.

The credibility of the hypothesis $A \in 2^\Theta$ is the sum of the masses of the elements that support it, while its plausibility is the sum of the masses of the elements that do not contradict it.

The credibility and plausibility functions are defined as:

$$\text{Bel}^\Theta(A) \triangleq \sum_{Y \subseteq A | Y \in 2^\Theta} m^\Theta(Y) \quad \text{and} \quad \text{Pl}^\Theta(A) \triangleq \sum_{Y \cap A \neq \emptyset | Y \in 2^\Theta} m^\Theta(Y).$$

5.3.3. *Non-additive measures and associated distributions*

The additivity axiom and probability measures

Probability theory aims to model the variability inherent in the phenomenon studied by associating a probability space $(\Omega, \mathcal{F}, \mathbb{P})$, where Ω defines the set of possible outcomes of the experiment, $\mathcal{F}$ the set of events (a tribe over Ω), and $\mathbb{P}: \mathcal{F} \to [0,1]$, a probability measure that provides the plausibility of each event.

A real random variable is a real variable X ; $(\Omega, \mathcal{F}) \to (\mathbb{R}, \mathcal{B}(\mathbb{R}))$ whose probability distribution $\mathbb{P}_X$ is the probability image measure $(\mathbb{R}, \mathcal{B}(\mathbb{R}))$ of $\mathbb{P}$, i.e. always a measurable application of $(\Omega, \mathcal{F}, \mathbb{P})$, over $\mathbb{R}$ and with its Borel set.

The additivity axiom of two events A and B – regardless of which two separate events belonging to the tribe T are considered – which are part of the reference space Ω, allows us to retrieve the classical probability measures. Neither the possibility measures nor the belief functions possessed this property.

DEFINITION.– *We define the probability distribution of X, noted as* $\mathbb{P}_X$*, as the image measure of* $\mathbb{P}$ *through X.*

When the variable is discrete, the distribution $\mathbb{P}_X$ includes point masses which are often represented in bar graphs or histograms.

DEFINITION.– *This probability distribution* $\mathbb{P}_X$ *makes it possible to define the cumulative distribution law F of a random variable X, as the application of* $\mathbb{R}$ *in* [0,1]:

$$F(X) = \mathbb{P}\,(X < x).$$

This allows us to calculate the probability of any interval over $\mathbb{R}$. It is a left-continuous monotonic function for any continuous variable.

DEFINITION.– *The density function f of the probability distribution* $\mathbb{P}_X$ *is defined if for any interval I of* $\mathbb{R}$:

$$\mathbb{P}_X(I) = \int_I f(x)dx = \int_{\mathbb{R}} \mathbb{I}_I(x)f(x)dx.$$

The cumulative distribution function F is differentiable, and it admits f as a derivative:

$$\mathbb{P}(a < X < b) = \int_a^b f(x)dx = F(b) - F(a)$$

Pre-measures and uncertain variables

DEFINITION.– *In line with how a random variable is defined, an uncertain variable is an application X defined on a confidence space* (Ω, T, m) *over* $\mathbb{R}$ *with its Borel set.*

The probability distribution of X is the pre-measure m_X over $\mathbb{R}$ defined by:

$$m_x(J) = m(\{\omega \in \Omega \mid X(\omega) \in J\}).$$

For any Borel part J of $\mathcal{B}(\mathbb{R})$ over $\mathbb{R}$.

DEFINITIONS.– *Possibility and necessity distribution.*

A possibility distribution is a function π of Ω in $[0,1]$ with a standardization condition:

$$\sup_{x \in \Omega} \pi(x) = 1.$$

If we consider the hypothesis of a closed world where at least one of the events is completely possible, a possibility distribution π makes it possible to establish a possibility measure through the formula:

$$\forall A \in C, \Pi(A) = \sup \{\pi(x), x \in A\}$$

Similarly, a possibility measure leads to a possibility distribution:

$$\forall x \in \Omega, \pi(x) = \Pi(\{x\}).$$

By duality, a necessity measure defines a possibility distribution[4]:

$$\forall A \in C, N(A) = 1 - \sup \{\pi(x), x \notin A\} = \inf\{1 - \pi(x), x \in A^C\}.$$

In the standardized case, $\Pi(\Omega) = 1$, so as to obtain

$$N(A) > 0 \Rightarrow \Pi(A) = 1 \text{ and } \Pi(A) < 1 \Rightarrow N(A) = 0.$$

Let us consider the value assigned to a variable X. Thus, Ω represents the variation range of this variable, and its possibility distribution the degrees to which each possible value can be assigned to the variable. The degree of membership of each value to the set of possible values (which defines a fuzzy set for this value) corresponds to the degree of possibility that this value will be assigned to the variable. The possibility distribution represents the imprecision of the value of the variable. Thus, a fuzzy number is a possibility distribution of the possible values that may be assigned to a number.

Therefore, let us reconsider the piezometric water level that can be found underground. Let Ω be the set of possible values (water level gauge). A possibility distribution over Ω defined for each object (point, region) may represent the possibility that each object has of reaching these water levels.

---

4 C is the set of the crisp sets of Ω.

Thus, we consider a possibility and a necessity in classical or crisp sets [BLO 04].

Let us consider a fuzzy subset A of Ω, the reference space, and its characteristic function μ of Ω in $[0,1]$, defined by $\{(x, \mu(x)), x \in A\}$. The notion of possibility is expanded by:

$$\Pi(\mu) = \sup_{x \in \Omega} \min(\mu(x), \pi(x)).$$

This is interpreted as follows: given a possibility distribution π over Ω, associated with the variable X, and taking its values in Ω, we assess to what extent "X is μ". Thus, the possibility of μ combines the degree to which the variable X is given its value x and the degree of membership of x to the fuzzy set.

A link between possibility, probabilities, and α-cuts

From any possibility distribution over π over $(\Omega, \mathcal{P}(\Omega))$, we can deduce the probability family:

$$\mathcal{P}(\pi) = \{\mathbb{P} | \forall A \subseteq \Omega, N(A) \le \mathbb{P}(A) \le \Pi(A)\}$$

where $\mathcal{P}$ is a family of probability measures over the measuring space. The pair (Π, N) corresponds to the boundaries $(\overline{\mathbb{P}}, \underline{\mathbb{P}})$ of $\mathcal{P}(\pi)$.

A family of cumulative distribution functions $F : X \to [0,1]$ is framed by the pair of functions $(\underline{F}, \overline{F})$, where $(\underline{F} \le \overline{F})$, extracted from π. This difference between the two functions reveals where there is imprecision, and the probability interval called P-box is the set of probability measures.

A possibility distribution π indicates the potential plausibility of the values of the parameter. It may be interpreted as a set of embedded confidence intervals, each with a specific degree of confidence $(E_i, v_i)_{i=1,...,k}$ and decreasing, where $(E_1 \subset E_2 \subset \cdots \subset E_k$ corresponds to the α_i-cuts $(v_2 < \cdots < v_k$ such that $v_i = 1 - \alpha_i)$. The data that include such pairs (interval, degree of confidence) allow us to establish a possibility distribution π over Ω through:

$$\forall \omega \in \Omega, \pi(\omega) = \min_{i=1,...,k} \max(\mathbb{1}_{E_i}(\omega), 1 - v_i).$$

Let us reconsider the introductory example. This is what an expert says about the possible values of the potential bearing capacity X of the bridge after the earthquake, over the reals:

– I am certain that $X \in [0.0,5.0]$;

– I am 60% sure that $X \in [1.0,4.0]$;

– I am 20% sure that $X \in [2.0,3.0]$.

The following figure – Figure 5.2 – represents the distribution induced by his opinion.

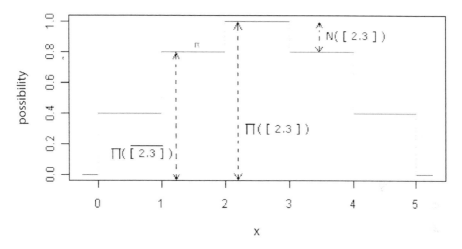

Figure 5.2. *Possibility distribution π induced by the opinion of an expert. For a color version of this figure, see www.iste.co.uk/batton/geographic1.zip*

In terms of probabilities, "I am 20% sure that $X \in [2.0,3.0]$" is interpreted as: the probability that $X \in [2.0,3.0]$ is at least equal to 0.2, or the probability that $X \notin [2.0,3.0]$ is at most equal to 0.8. The two boundaries – upper and lower – which frame the probability of the event $X \in [2.0,3.0]$, are the following:

– a degree of possibility $\Pi([2.0,3.0]) = 1$;

– a degree of necessity $N([2.0,3.0]) = 0.2$.

The link between belief functions and possibilities

For a possibility distribution $\pi: \Omega \to [0,1]$, the α-cut of π is the interval $F_\alpha = \{x | \mu_F(x) \geq \alpha\}$. If the d values of α are hypothetically sampled according to a uniform distribution of the embedded sets (which include the d α-cuts $F_{\alpha d}$ and the elementary masses $m_d = \alpha_d - \alpha_{d+1}$ with $\alpha_1 = 1$ and $\alpha_{dmax+1} = 0$, $\pi(x)$ is defined as:

$$\pi(x) = \Sigma_{x \in F_{\alpha d}} m_d .$$

Similarly, regarding the set Ω as the frame of discernment, a mass function $m^\Omega(.)$ can be obtained according to the α-cut principle (Figure 5.3). The focal elements are the mass α-cuts $F_{\alpha d}$:

$$m^\Omega(F_{\alpha d}) = m_d .$$

Thus, [DUB 88] established the relationships between possibility distribution, probability family, and belief mass, which are outlined in the following figure:

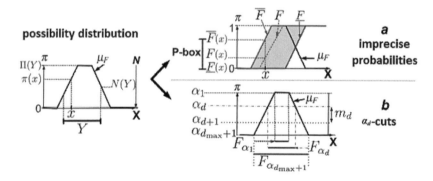

Figure 5.3. *From a possibility distribution π to belief masses through α-cuts and imprecise probabilities (in [CAR 17]). For a color version of this figure, see www.iste.co.uk/batton/geographic1.zip*

5.3.4. *Tools used to manipulate fuzzy measures and sets*

In the context of spatial analysis, it is often necessary to simultaneously combine attribute measures of a geographic object and geometric measures of the object through its adopted geometric model (vector or raster). Thus, it is necessary to introduce combination operators that imply membership or possibility distribution functions which characterize the imperfection of the fuzzy object.

After recontextualizing the set operations defined over these fuzzy sets, our goal will be to present the mathematical functions that make it possible to define some set operations for keeping these membership properties. Operators such as t-norms and t-conorms can introduce aggregation operators such as averages, in particular, the sums implied in merge operators.

We also provide some theoretical elements about Bayesian and possibilistic conditioning as well as Zadeh's extension principle, since they constitute the foundations for the reasoning processes presented in Chapter 3. We have chosen to present some elements succinctly since our aim is to illustrate in basic terms how this type of information is employed in the context of geographic information (in particular, the probabilistic framework is not developed except for some points that can be reconsidered in reasoning processes introduced later).

5.3.4.1. *Fuzzy set operations*

[ZAD 76] defined fuzzy set operations such as the equality of two fuzzy sets, the inclusion of a fuzzy set, and the intersection and union of fuzzy sets.

The equality of two fuzzy sets is defined by the equality of their membership functions:

$$\mu = v \Leftrightarrow \forall x \in \Omega, \mu(x) = v(x).$$

The inclusion of a fuzzy set into another is defined by an inequality between the membership functions:

$$\mu \subseteq v \Leftrightarrow \forall x \in \Omega, \mu(x) \leq v(x).$$

The intersection of two fuzzy sets is defined by the minimum point-by-point between the membership functions. The union of two fuzzy sets is defined by the maximum point-by-point between the membership functions:

$$\forall x \in \Omega, \mu \cap v = \min[\mu(x), v(x)]$$

$$\forall x \in \Omega, \mu \cup v = \max[\mu(x), v(x)].$$

The complement of a fuzzy set is defined by:

$$\forall x \in \Omega, \mu^C(x) = 1 - \mu(x).$$

These operations are in line with set operations. However, some properties that are verified in the binary case, like the law of excluded middle and that of non-contradiction, no longer apply. In general, for two fuzzy sets, we obtain:

$$\mu \cup \mu^C \neq \Omega, \text{ and } \mu \cap \mu^C \neq \emptyset.$$

5.3.4.2. *Fuzzy set operators*

Operators combine the degrees of possibility or membership to the same point of Ω. They act on this set point-by-point so that they are defined as functions either over $[0,1]$ or over $[0,1] \times [0,1]$. Among other things, this introduction makes it possible to use some operators to review beliefs and plausibilities in the third part of this book.

DEFINITION.– *A triangular norm (or* t-*norm) is a function* $t: [0,1] \times [0,1] \rightarrow [0,1]$ *such that*:

1. t is commutative: $\forall (x,y) \in [0,1]^2, \ t(x,y) = t(y,x)$[5];

2. t is associative : $\forall (x,y) \in [0,1]^2, \ t[t(x,y),z] = t[x,t(y,z),z]$;

3. 1 is a neutral element: $\forall x \in [0,1], t(x,1) = t(1,x) = x$;

4. t is increasing (monotonicity): $\forall (x,x',y,y') \in [0,1]^4, \ (x \leq x' et \ y \leq y' \ \Rightarrow t(x,y) \leq t(x',y'))$.

DEFINITION.– *A* t-*conorm is a function* $T: [0,1] \times [0,1] \rightarrow [0,1]$ *such that*:

1. t is commutative: $\forall (x,y) \in [0,1]^2, \ T(x,y) = T(y,x)$;

2. t is associative: $\forall (x,y) \in [0,1]^2, \ T[T(x,y),z] = T[x,T(y,z),z]$;

3. 0 is a neutral element: $\forall x \in [0,1], T(x,0) = T(0,x) = x$;

4. T is increasing (monotonicity): $\forall (x,x',y,y') \in [0,1]^5, \ (x \leq x' and \ y \leq y' \ \Rightarrow T(x,y) \leq T(x',y'))$.

The operators $\min(x,y)$, xy, and $\max(0, x+y-1)$ are the most commonly used t-norms. The t-norms are appropriate for set operators that

---

5 The values to combine – x, y, etc. – represent the degrees of membership or possibility defined over $[0,1]$.

are used for proposition intersection and conjunction, as a t-norm verifies that for any pair $(x, y) \in [0,1]$, $t(x, y) \le x$ and $t(x, y) \le y$. This guarantees that any t-norm will be smaller or equal to the operator $\min(x, y)$. This also respects the condition that an element cannot belong more strongly to the intersection of two fuzzy subsets than it belongs to one or the other.

The operators $\max(x, y)$, $x + y - xy$, and $\min(1, x + y)$ are the most commonly used t-conorms. The t-conorms are appropriate for union (and "or" logic) set operators, since a t-conorm verifies that for any pair $(x, y) \in [0,1]$, $T(x, y) \ge x$ and $T(x, y) \ge y$. This guarantees that any t-conorm will be greater or equal to the operator $\max(x, y)$. This also respects the condition that an element may belong more strongly to the union of the two fuzzy subsets than it belongs to one or the other.

Table 5.1 provides some examples of t-norms and t-conorms.

	Zadeh	Probabilistic	Lukasiewicz
t-norm	$\min(x, y)$	xy	$\max(0, x + y - 1)$
t-conorm	$\max(x, y)$	$x + y - xy$	$\min(1, x + y)$

Table 5.1. *Examples of* t-norms *and* t-conorms *used in the frame of spatial objects*

DEFINITION.– *Averaging operators.*

An averaging operator is a function $g: [0,1] \times [0,1] \to [0,1]$ whose result $g(x, y)$ is always included between *min* and *max*. g is commutative and increasing in relation to the two variables. The idempotency property $g(x, x) = x$ is verified, but in general, this operator is not associative, except for the median.

The averages are continuous and strictly increasing as:

$$\forall (x, y) \in [0,1]^2, \; g(x, y) = k^{-1} \left[\frac{k(x) + k(y)}{2} \right].$$

For functions $k(x)$, where $\alpha \in \mathbb{R}$, of the kind: $\forall x \in [0,1], k(x) = x^{\alpha}$, we can identify the classical averages, which are:

– arithmetic mean: $\alpha = 1$, $g(x, y) = \frac{x+y}{2}$;

– quadratic mean: $\alpha = 2$, $g(x,y) = \sqrt{\frac{x^2+y^2}{2}}$;

– harmonic mean: $\alpha = -1$, $g(x,y) = \frac{2xy}{x+y}$;

– geometric mean: $\alpha = 0$, $g(x,y) = \sqrt{xy}$;

– the limit value, $g(x,y)$, tends toward the min when $\alpha \rightarrow -\infty$ and toward the max when $\alpha \rightarrow +\infty$.

Fuzzy weighted and integral means (Choquet and Sugeno integrals) belong to this class of averaging operators. When self-duality is respected, the sum operator becomes symmetrical. As a result, a change in value scale does not modify the nature of the combination. It should be pointed out that classical aggregation methods are unsymmetrical and sensitive to scale change and inversion. Operators that involve conflict, in particular, will be examined later among digital merge methods.

5.3.4.3. *Some theoretical elements: the extension principle and the conditioning principle*

THEOREM.– *The extension principle.*

[ZAD 76] introduced the extension principle alongside the notion of the set [ZAD 65]. If A is a fuzzy subset of the universe X and an application, $f: X \rightarrow Y$, then the goal is to construct the images of A through f. This fundamental principle makes it possible to apply mathematical functions for imprecise values to the fuzzy subsets of $\mathbb{R}$.

DEFINITION.– *Let A be a fuzzy subset of the universe X and an application $f: X \rightarrow Y$, $f(A)$. The extension theorem can define a fuzzy subset B of the universe Y associated with A through f. $f(A)$ is a fuzzy set defined over Y.*

$$\forall y \in Y, \mu_B(y) = \begin{cases} \sup_{\{x \in X | y = f(x)\}} \mu_A(x) & \text{if } f^{-1}(y) \neq 0 \\ 0 & \text{if } f^{-1}(y) = 0 \end{cases}$$

If f is injective, this equation is reduced to:

$$\forall y \in Y, \mu_B(y) = \begin{cases} 0 & \text{if } f^{-1}(y) = 0 \\ \mu_A[f^{-1}(y)] & \text{otherwise} \end{cases}$$

The application of the extension principle to such operations on fuzzy numbers as addition, multiplication, etc. – thus, any operation * on two fuzzy numbers – is defined by:

$$\forall z \in \mathbb{R}, \mu_{A*B}(z) = \sup_{(x,y)\in\mathbb{R}^2|x*y=z} \min[\mu_A(x), \mu_B(x)].$$

The extension of a commutative operation is commutative, just like associativity. Calculations that involve L-R fuzzy numbers use the boundaries of each interval.

Conditional probabilities

Whether in the context of possibilities or probabilities, knowledge about the possible states of the world only depends on present knowledge or hypotheses that may be established around an event A and its membership to the universe Ω.

Naturally, taking into consideration the supplementary knowledge of a fact C (new information), the occurrence of the event A in a hypothetical context where C is true (where it can be associated with a bet on A), or the reassessment of the probability of A when the event C has taken place will change the confidence measures of the possible states. Thus, passing from a probability to a so-called conditional probability involves re-standardizing the probabilities assigned to the states of C. Let $P(A)$ be the probability of A and the new context $C \sqsubset \Omega$. The probability A in this new context is noted as $P(A|C)$, and it is equal to: $P(A|C) = \frac{P(A \cap C)}{P(C)}$.

THEOREM.– *Bayes' theorem.*

If $\{C_1, ..., C_k\}$ *forms a partition of* Ω, *then* $P(A) = \sum_{i=1}^{k} P(A|C_i)P(C_i)$; Bayes' theorem:

$$P(C_j|A) = \frac{P(A|C_j)P(C_j)}{\sum_{i=1}^{k} P(A|C_i)P(C_i)}.$$

The conditioning of non-additive representations: the case of possibilities

We can recall the following formula, which expresses the choice of the less informative solution when the two events differ from the empty set:

$$\Pi(A|C) = 1 \text{ if } \Pi(A \cap C) = \Pi(C) \text{ and } \Pi(A \cap C) \quad \text{otherwise.}$$

5.4. *Spatial objects*

Here, we tackle the issues that concern the spatial representation of a geographic object whose definition, as part of its geographic acquisition, must incorporate the fuzziness or uncertainty of its geometry.

Broad boundary objects involve representing in Euclidean geometry not only a polygon-like spatial entity whose imprecision concerns the identification of the inclusive certain and uncertain areas of the object but also polylines. The way in which a geographic point belongs to a spatial object (in the semantic sense of the area) is also presented as a degree of membership to a set through spatial fuzzy objects.

5.4.1. *Broad boundary objects*

The so-called egg-yolk theory [COH 96] introduces the concept of broad boundary spatial regions. In fact, this type of spatial region, called "vague" [BEJ 09a, PIN 10], includes two regions: an inner region (the "yolk") surrounded by an external region (the "white"). The yolk region is a certain part of an object. The white region is the uncertain part, which corresponds to the uncertain boundary of the object (see Figure 5.4). These two regions are adjacent, and their union constitutes "the egg", i.e. the vague object. [CLE 97] suggested a model similar to the egg-yolk model but defined it in slightly different terms. In this model, a vague region A includes two simple regions A1 and A2; A2 is spatially included in A1. The difference between A1 and A2 yields the uncertain part. A1 is the maximum extension of the object, while A2 is its minimum extension [BEJ 09a, BEJ 09b].

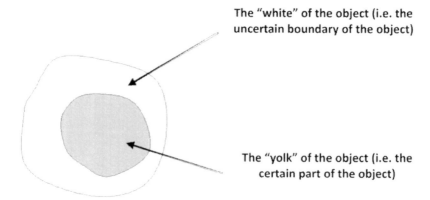

The "white" of the object (i.e. the uncertain boundary of the object)

The "yolk" of the object (i.e. the certain part of the object)

Figure 5.4. *A vague spatial region according to the egg-yolk model*

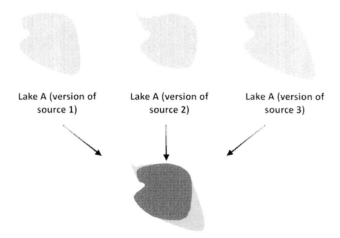

The integrated version of Lake A (represented as a vague region)

Figure 5.5. *The integrated version of Lake A (represented as a vague region). For a color version of this figure, see www.iste.co.uk/batton/geographic1.zip*

A broad boundary object may be produced by integrating several distinct representations of the same phenomenon. Figure 5.5 shows an example. Some representations of the same lake are available in three different sources. The differences in the representations of the lake may have various origins. A wide boundary consensus representation can be obtained very easily. The spatial union of the three representations yields the maximum extension of the lake. The spatial intersection of the three representations yields the minimum extension of the lake.

The boundaries of a line are often defined as its two end points [EGE 90]. Thus, a wide boundary line may, for example, be defined as a line that has a surface region at each of its ends [BEJ 09a, BEJ 09b]. This type of object can reveal that there is some uncertainty about the endpoints of the line. The end points are known to be included in these surface regions, but their exact position within the regions is unknown. Figure 5.6 illustrates this type of representation.

Figure 5.6. *A wide boundary line*

5.4.2. *Fuzzy objects*

In a broad boundary representation model, a point in space belongs, or perhaps does not belong, or maybe belongs, to a spatial object. To measure the degree of membership of a point to a spatial object, the fuzzy subset theory put forward by [ZAD 65] is often employed. As previously stated, a fuzzy subset A of Ω is an application of Ω over the interval [0,1]. A membership function μ_A assigns to each element $x \in$ of Ω a real number in [0,1]. $\mu_{A(x)}$ is the degree of membership of x in A.

Figure 5.7. *A visual representation of fuzzy spatial regions*

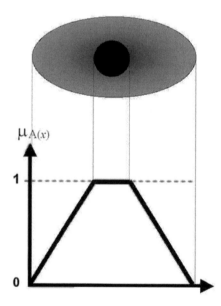

Figure 5.8. *The membership function of a fuzzy spatial region*

A fuzzy subset may be used to model a fuzzy spatial region [DIL 16, SCH 01]. According to this type of formalism, a fuzzy region is represented by a membership function. Any point in space is associated with a degree of membership to the region included in the interval [0,1]. A point belongs to this region in relation to this degree. If a point in space is assigned a degree equal to 1, then it certainly belongs to a spatial object. If a point has a degree of 0, then it does not belong to the object. Figure 5.7 shows a visual representation of two fuzzy spatial regions. As can be seen in the figure, the darker the color is, the closer the degree is to 1 (i.e. certainty). Figure 5.8 plots the membership function of a fuzzy region and shows the correspondence with the region in question. The core of A is the certain part of the region (in black).

Some α-cuts may also be used. Figure 5.9 shows an example of this type of model. This representation can be reduced to the identification of a set of crisp (i.e. classical) regions embedded in one another. Each region r_i is associated with a threshold. Each point of r_i has a degree that is greater or equal to this threshold.

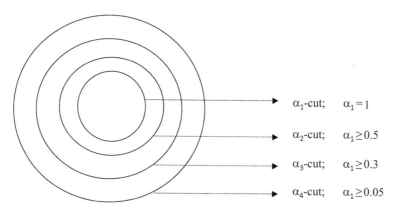

Figure 5.9. *Fuzzy spatial regions represented by a set of α-cuts*

5.5. Reconsidering the introductory examples

The three examples introduced at the beginning of this chapter made it possible to outline where and how the imperfection, imprecision, and uncertainty of geographic objects can be deciphered. The formalisms of the theories related to the representation of uncertainty provide a formal and universal language that translates this way of qualifying imprecision. Besides, they make it possible to accurately distinguish: the object, parameter, or phenomenon studied, the attribute that assigns one or more values to an object, and the confidence regarded as a reliability index of a piece of information.

Reconsidering the first example

The first example concerns the following fact: the condition of a bridge in a district hit by an earthquake. The issue is formalizing the information available about the bridge: it is possible to focus simultaneously on the geographic (geolocation), semantic, and functional components of the bridge. In a classic GIS program, the object *Bridge* is classically viewed through the operations of this object class whose attribute table can contain the attribute "exists" or "is damaged", "functional". In a certain case, the values of each attribute can provide information on whether the bridge exists (Boolean), 10% of it is damaged, or 95% of it is functional. However, this can only be true if the related information is associated with a certain and observable or assessable fact.

In an uncertain framework, the information available is:

– Either the bridge still exists, or it no longer exists. The fact "the bridge exists" and the fact "the bridge no longer exists" are completely unknown. Uncertainty concerns various precise values which may be associated with a certain level of confidence, taking into consideration the scale of the earthquake and observations. An exclusive and binary type of confidence of the kind "yes", "no", and the possibly "yes or no", applied to the total lack of knowledge about the attribute "exists" can structure this information. A probability would no longer assign a binary value to the fact "the bridge exists" but a degree of confidence, the probability p. The probability of the confidence assigned to the complementary event "the bridge no longer exists" is $(1-p)$.

– The bridge may still exist, but the expert is not sure. This is a case of partial ignorance. In these circumstances, the possibility theory can represent the possibility of an elementary event "the bridge exists" as $\Pi(x) = 1$ for an unsurprising event with a certainty value of at least 0.15. Therefore, this corresponds to a necessity measure of $N(x) = 0.15$. These two boundaries frame the probability of the event "the bridge exists". On the contrary, the fact "the bridge no longer exists" (the complementary fact) may not be surprising after an earthquake, yielding a possibility of $\Pi(x) = 0.8$ but without certainty $N(x) = 0$.

– The fact is certain – the bridge exists – but its precise position is unknown. A classic representation model of the position (x,y) frames it through coordinate intervals [**x;y**]. Between these boundaries, the point is certain. However, GISs cannot easily deal with this mode of representation, except when regarding the position of the point as an elementary surface region. Introducing a fuzzy region model can measure the membership of a point to the spatial region (cf. the previous paragraph). The simultaneous combination of the uncertainty about the fact "the bridge exists" and about its spatial and geometric component "position" involves manipulating various tools and formalisms. Part III will present a review of the ways of qualifying the geographic information.

Reconsidering the second example

The geographic object is a piezometric field. What the researchers want to find out is the quantity produced by a well whose position is known [the point (x,y) in the geographic space]. The unknown is the quantity of water produced. An expert will estimate it to range between [5; 10] m^3/h and with a certainty of 50%. Thus, a possibility distribution can incorporate an expert opinion about the possible values of the quantity of water and the necessity about the certainty it assigns to each value. Thus, the expert delimits a family of quantitative probabilities, thanks to their qualitative assessment. A hydrological simulation tool can estimate these water resources (deterministic flow code): the quantity in question is a random variable, estimated through redundant (Monte Carlo) simulations and associated with an *a posteriori* probability distribution and a distribution of its confidence interval. In this case, the values will be known with a degree of reliability related to their estimate. Thus, we will now refer to uncertainty instead of imprecision. For a given well, the presentation of the attribute information in the GIS will resemble that suggested in the first example.

Reconsidering the third example

A parcel of land may be classically viewed as a polygon in a vector model. It delimits a finite surface on the planisphere. To reconstruct some land-cover parcels, the data image sent by satellites measures some fields of the detected wavelengths. Passing from continuous to vector data requires, on one hand, the detection of the boundary between two areas and the type of land cover in relation to the response recorded. If the type of parcel is progressive, or if its detection is tricky, the boundary of the parcel will be vague or imprecise. In a point in space, a membership function $\mu(A)$ is associated with a type-A parcel. The fuzzy spatial region representation is appropriate. However, the association between a point in space and the function of its membership to this region requires a means of storing and manipulating this continuous function. The representation mode that employs a set of α-cuts (Figure 5.9) is compatible with the vector mode of GISs, even if generalizing to one cover is not easy. The set of points, whose degree of membership is equal to 1, form not only the certain and so-called "egg-yolk" part but also the core of the related possibility distribution.

5.6. References

[BEJ 09a] BEJAOUI L., Qualitative topological relationships for objects with possibly vague shapes: implications on the specification of topological integrity constraints in transactional spatial databases and in spatial data warehouses, Thesis, Université Blaise Pascal (Clermont Ferrand)/Université Laval, Quebec, Canada, 2009.

[BEJ 09b] BEJAOUI L., PINET F., BÉDARD Y. *et al.*, "Qualified topological relations between spatial objects with possible vague shape", *International Journal of Geographical Information Science*, vol. 23, no. 7, pp. 877–921, 2009.

[BLO 04] BLOCH I., MAITRE H., Les méthodes de raisonnement dans les images, Report, Brique VOIR – RASIM, ENST TELECOM PARIS, Paris, France, 2004.

[BOU 09] BOUYSSOU D., DUBOIS D., PIRLOT M. *et al.*, *Decision-making Process: Concepts and Methods*, ISTE Ltd, London, UK, and John Wiley & Sons, New York, USA, 2009.

[CAR 17] CARLADOUS S., Approche intégrée d'aide à la décision basée sur la propagation de l'imperfection de l'information – application à l'efficacité des mesures de protection torrentielle, PhD thesis, Université de Lyon, Ecole des Mines de Saint-Etienne, France, 2017.

[CLE 97] CLEMENTINI E., DI FELICE P., "Approximate Topological Relations", *International Journal of Approximate Reasoning*, vol. 16, no. 2, pp. 173–204, 1997.

[COH 96] COHN A.G., GOTTS N.M., "The 'egg-yolk' representation of regions with indeterminate boundaries", in BURROUGH P. and FRANK A.U. (eds), *Geographic Objects with Indeterminate Boundaries,* Taylor and Francis, London, UK, pp. 171–187, 1996.

[DIL 16] DILO A., Representation of and reasoning with vagueness in spatial information: a system for handling vague objects, PhD Thesis, Wageningen University, ITC Publication, Enschede, The Netherlands, 2016.

[DUB 88] DUBOIS D., PRADE H., "Representation and combination of uncertainty with belief functions and possibility measures", *Computational Intelligence Journal*, vol. 4, no. 3, pp. 244–264, September 1988.

[EGE 90] EGENHOFER M., HERRING J., Categorizing binary topological relations between regions, lines, and points in geographic databases, Report, Department of Surveying Engineering, University of Maine, Orono, ME, USA, 1990.

[PAR 01] PARSONS S., *Qualitative Methods for Reasoning under Uncertainty*, The MIT Press, UK, 2001.

[PIN 10] PINET F., Modélisation des contraintes d'intégrité dans les systèmes d'information environnementaux, HDR, Université Blaise Pascal, Paris, France, available at: http://motive.cemagref.fr/_publication/PUB00028995.pdf, 2010.

[SCH 01] SCHNEIDER M., "A design of topological predicates for complex crisp and fuzzy regions", in KUNII H.S., JAJODIA S., SØLVBERG A. (eds), *Conceptual Modeling – ER 2001*, Lecture Notes in Computer Science, Springer, Berlin, Germany, vol. 2224, pp. 103–116, 2001.

[SHA 76] SHAFER G., *A Mathematical Theory of Evidence*, Princeton University Press, Princeton, NJ, 1976.

[ZAD 65] ZADEH L.A., "Fuzzy sets", *Information and Control Journal*, vol. 8, no. 3, pp. 338–353, June 1965.

[ZAD 76] ZADEH L.A., "A fuzzy-algorithmic approach to the definition of complex or imprecise concepts", in *Systems Theory in the Social Sciences*, Springer, Birkhäuser, Basel, Switzerland, pp. 202–288, 1976.

6

Representing Diagrams of Imperfect Geographic Objects

6.1. Introduction

Theoretical representations based on diagrams are commonly used as a methodological tool to visually describe the main structure of a system, computer programs, or a database. UML (Unified Modeling Language) [BOO 99] has become indispensable for the description of these diagrams.

Over time, various means of simplifying the description of geographic objects in UML diagrams have been suggested [PIN 10a], [PIN 10b]. Here, we will define one of the most common visual formalisms used to describe classes of spatial objects, namely, PVL (Plug-in for Visual Language) as well as its extension for models of imperfect objects.

6.2. Describing the theoretical models of geographic objects

We will first describe the main standard notations in UML, as well as the notations that result from a UML extension employed for the representation of spatiotemporal objects. The UML extension for the spatial dimension used here is called PVL. It was introduced by Bédard [BED 99] and implemented in a tool called Perceptory [BED 04]. We will use the example illustrated in Figure 6.1 to present these elements. The UML model in this figure represents various types of geographic objects that can be found in a

Chapter written by François PINET and Cyril DE RUNZ.

city. It illustrates that, in a city, there may be buildings, roads, parks, and different types of vehicles that are driven on these roads.

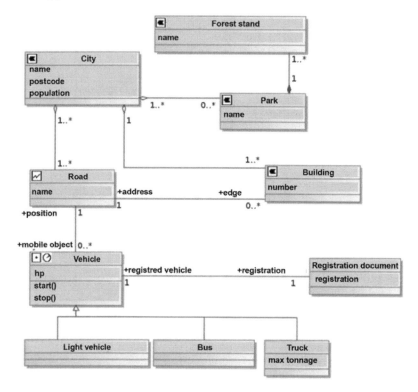

Figure 6.1. *A UML-PVL model*

The main standard notations in UML are the following:

Classes. Classes are represented by rectangles. Each class corresponds to a type of object that we wish to model (City, Road, Park, Forest Stand, etc.). Classes have attributes and operations. Attributes are variables. For example, a city has the attributes, name, postcode and population. Operations are features enabled by the objects of these classes. For instance, a vehicle may start or stop.

Simple associations. Classes are linked to one another by associations. By tracing these associations, a model designer defines semantic links among classes. In Figure 6.1, the classes Vehicle and Registration document are linked by the association "registered vehicle ... registration" so as to indicate that the registration of a vehicle is shown in its registration document.

Association multiplicities. These are numbers specified at each end of an association. These multiplicities reveal the numbers of objects involved in the association. For example, the multiplicities of the association "address ... edge," which links Road and Building, indicate that:

– Each building is associated with one road (multiplicity "1");

– Each road is associated with a number ranging from 0 to N buildings, where $N > 0$ (multiplicity " 0..*"). The asterisk corresponds to a variable number > 0.

The multiplicities of the association "registered vehicle ... registration" reveal that each vehicle has a registration document and that each document corresponds to a vehicle.

Composition associations. These associations are represented by a black diamond. It is an association that possesses specific semantics, a "whole-parts" type of association: a whole is formed by a set of parts. A diamond is drawn beside a class that corresponds to the whole. For instance, each park includes a forest stand. In this type of association, if the whole ceases to exist, the parts will necessarily be destroyed.

Aggregation associations. These associations are represented by a white diamond. They share the same semantics as compositions, with the only difference that the parts will not necessarily be destroyed if the whole ceases to exist. For example, Figure 6.1 indicates that cities are aggregations of roads, buildings, and parks. If a city ceases to exist, buildings, roads, and parks may survive – this could be the case if a city disappears after several districts are merged (in case of re-demarcation). Choosing to use compositions or aggregations significantly depends on the end-of-life scenarios of the objects that we wish to consider in a model.

Generalization–specialization relationships. These inheritance relationships, represented by triangles, establish hierarchies among classes. For example, the class Truck specializes the class Vehicle (and Vehicle generalizes Truck). Trucks inherit all the attributes, operations, and associations of vehicles, but they may also have specific properties (max tonnage).

Here are some PVL notations used to represent the spatiotemporal aspects of the objects [BED 99]:

The dimension of the spatial objects. A symbol specifies the dimension of the spatial objects of each class. The icons ⊡, ◼, ☑ represent 0D (point), 1D (linear), and 2D (area) objects respectively. In Figure 6.1, we have chosen a point representation for the position of the vehicles, a linear representation for the roads, and an area representation for the edges of the cities, parks, buildings and forest stands.

The temporality of the spatial objects. Using the symbol ⊘ besides a spatial symbol indicates that the spatial evolution of an object must be tracked in the system modeled. Figure 6.1 points out that the objects belonging to the class Vehicle can track the history of all their positions over time.

Thus, these diagrams can represent in simple terms models that will be implemented in databases, programs, etc. PVL diagrams may be transformed in classical UML diagrams (i.e. without symbols), entailing an increase in the number of classes and associations of the diagram. In fact, in classical UML, for example, the classes that include point, linear, and area objects can be defined and linked to the other classes of the diagram by association. It is also possible to add "geometry" attributes to classes in order to store geographic objects. The complex type of these attributes makes it possible to store the form and position of the objects. As for the implementation of the diagrams, if we consider the translation of a PVL diagram into a relational database, the classes will be replaced by tables. Various storage structures for geographic objects may be used depending on the target database management system.

6.3. Describing the theoretical models of imperfect geographic objects

The F-Perceptory model, introduced by [ZOG 13], [ZOG 16] and expanded by [KHA 17a], [KHA 17b], [KHA 17c], puts forward an extension inspired on one hand by PVL diagrams and on the other, by suggestions on how to characterize fuzziness in UML models.

[MA 11] introduced some fuzzy extensions for most UML concepts: classes, attributes, relationships, generalization and dependence. The extended model is called Fuzzy UML and makes up for the semantic limitations encountered in UML when managing imperfection by representing fuzzy classes surrounded by dotted frames.

Relying on these principles, Zoghlami [ZOG 13] has suggested the use of symbols to represent imprecise and, more particularly, fuzzy, spatial, and temporal components. For example, the symbol ▦ corresponds to a fuzzy area object. The symbol ◔ corresponds to a fuzzy date, i.e. a date associated with a degree of membership. The authors in [ZOG 16] have put forward representations based on class diagrams of fuzzy geographic objects that are simple in spatial shape (fuzzy point objects, fuzzy linear objects, and fuzzy area objects).

The F-Perceptory approach is centered on a UML model of fuzzy regions that employs α-cut discretization (see Chapter 5). This approach includes three strong constraints that must be verified to consider the integrity of a representation: (1) at least two α-cuts must be involved; (2) the α-cuts must be linked and standardized (only one α-cut must have a degree of membership equal to 1); (3) the α-cuts must be embedded in one another (those with lower degrees of membership containing those with higher degrees of membership).

On a general level, Figure 6.2 [ZOG 13] shows how a class A with a fuzzy region symbol ▦ can be transformed into a classical UML diagram.

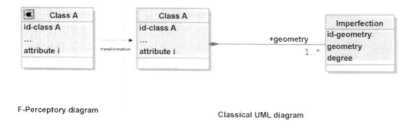

F-Perceptory diagram

Classical UML diagram

Figure 6.2. *Passing from F-Perceptory to classical UML*

In the classical UML version, an imperfection class is added to store each α-cut. For example, in order to store the fuzzy region in Figure 5.9 (Chapter 5), the objects of the class Imperfection could correspond to those shown in Table 6.1. Each region corresponds to the geographic area of each of the four α-cuts. The degree corresponds to the external boundary of each region.

Imperfection

Id-geometry	Geometry	Degree	Id-class A
1	◯	1	A1
2	◯	0.5	A1
3	◯	0.3	A1
4	◯	0.05	A1

Table 6.1. *Objects that belong to the class Imperfection*

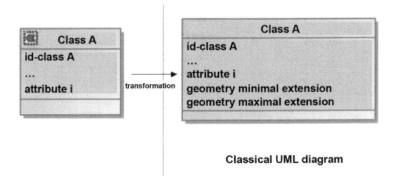

Figure 6.3. *Passing from a broad boundary region to classical UML*

It is also possible to describe broad boundary objects in UML in a simple way. Suppose that the symbol in Figure 6.3 corresponds this time to a broad boundary region. The figure shows how it is possible to pass from a simplified representation based on symbols to a classical UML representation. It reveals that the symbol is replaced by two geographic attributes that make it possible to store the spatial coordinates of the minimum and maximum extensions of the objects.

6.4. Toward massive databases

Big data management has led to the appearance of new non-relational data management systems called NoSQL. These systems focus on the scaling and performance limitations [BOR 12] of relational database management systems by relaxing the ACID properties and distributing processes. The so-called ACID properties (atomicity, consistency, isolation, and durability) define the execution quality of a digital transaction. They are at the core of RDBMS.

NoSQL systems, such as Cassandra and MongoDB, manage geospatial data. Within the context of the F-Perceptory approach, a system has been put forward to enable the management of fuzzy geographic data in these systems [KHA 17a], [KHA 17b], [KHA 17c].

The working principle of the system involves firstly the introduction of a light schema, called Fuzzy-GeoJSON. It is then used to structure data compatible with the GeoJSON format, and some data validation phases aimed at respecting the set of constraints related to the objects characterized by fuzzy spatial components in the context of F-Perceptory modeling.

Within this framework, in addition to the Fuzzy-GeoJSON schema Khalifi, de Runz and Faiz [KHA 17a], [KHA 17b], [KHA 17c] have suggested some format validation algorithms. Generally, these algorithms have a complexity in $O(n\ (m\ +\ m2))$, where n is the number of objects and m the maximum number of α-cuts by objects. Due to the interpretability and production costs of the data, a large m value is not necessarily relevant (since $m = 7$ is already a large number for the interpretation of the results). Thus, the complexity of the verification stage may be regarded as linear, and it is in keeping with Big data management [KHA 17a], [KHA 17b], [KHA 17c].

6.5. References

[BED 99] BÉDARD Y., "Visual modelling of spatial database towards spatial PVL and UML", *Geomatica*, vol. 53, no. 2, pp. 169–185, 1999.

[BED 04] BÉDARD Y., LARRIVEE S. , PROULX M.J. *et al.* "Modeling geospatial databases with plug-ins for visual languages: a pragmatic approach and the impacts of 16 years of research and experimentations on perceptory", *Lecture Notes in Computer Science*, vol. 3289, pp. 17–30, 2004.

[BOO 99] BOOCH G., RUMBAUGH J., JACOBSON I., *The Unified Modeling Language User Guide*, Addison-Wesley, Reading, MA, 1999.

[BOR 12] BORKAR V.R., CAREY M.J., LI, C., "Big data platforms: what's next?", *XRDS*, vol. 19, no. 1, pp. 44–49, 2012.

[KHA 17a] KHALFI B., Modélisation et construction des bases de données géographiques floues et maintien de la cohérence de modèles pour les SGBD SQL et NoSQL, PhD thesis, co-tutelage Paris 8-Tunis, 2017.

[KHA 17b] KHALFI B., DE RUNZ C., FAIZ S., "A new methodology for storing consistent fuzzy geospatial data in Big Data environment", *IEEE Transactions on Big Data*, 2017.

[KHA 17c] KHALFI B., DE RUNZ C., FAIZ S., "Extending F-Perceptory to model fuzzy objects with composite geometries for GIS", *Transactions in GIS*, vol. 21, no. 6, pp. 1364–1378, 2017.

[MA 11] MA Z., ZHANG F., YAN L., "Fuzzy information modeling in UML class diagram and relational database models", *Applied Soft Computing*, vol. 11, no. 6, pp. 4236–4245, 2011.

[PIN 10a] PINET F., "Entity-relationship and object-oriented formalisms for modeling spatial environmental data", *Environmental Modelling & Software*, vol. 30, pp. 80–91, 2010.

[PIN 10b] PINET F., "Un point sur les formalismes ER et OO pour les systèmes d'information spatiale", *Revue Internationale de Géomatique*, vol. 20, no. 4, pp. 399–428, 2010.

[ZOG 13] ZOGHLAMI A., Modélisation et conception de systèmes d'information géographique gérant l'imprécision, PhD thesis, Paris, 2013.

[ZOG 16] ZOGHLAMI A., DE RUNZ C., AKDAG H., "F-perceptory: an approach for handling fuzziness of spatiotemporal data in geographical databases", *International Journal of Spatial, Temporal and Multimedia Information Systems*, vol. 1, no. 1, pp. 30–62, 2016.

Part 3

Reasoning and Treatment

Algebraic Reasoning for Uncertain Data

7.1. Introduction

In this part, we will present some spatial reasoning models based on algebras. First, we will introduce the notion of algebra, showing how this mathematical tool has been employed to formalize and manipulate relationships about time and then space. Afterward, we will present the lattice formalism that allows us to view the reasoning process carried out in relation to algebras. Finally, we will examine some sets of relations for fuzzy spatial objects on which algebraic reasoning can be used.

To illustrate our goal, we consider, as an example, a classification problem concerning farmland based on satellite images [BAC 04], [LEB 07a]. The classification is carried out according to pre-established diagrams that have been qualitatively described by expert agronomists. Figure 7.1 illustrates a diagram of this kind besides an excerpt from a satellite image that may correspond to it. The image has been segmented and labeled according to various land-cover classes shown in different colors (built areas, corn, wheat, permanent grassland, temporary grassland, various types of forest, etc.). Unrecognized or irrelevant areas are shown in black. The diagram shows objects that represent various types of land cover (towns, pens, grasslands, crops) and morphological information (plateaus, valleys). It can be interpreted as follows: *the village is situated in a valley at the bottom of the plateau; the built area has an elongated shape, the village site has a linear structure and a fairly rectangular shape; it is surrounded on both sides by the state forest; the crop plots are situated between the built area*

Chapter written by Florence LE BER.

and the state forest, but asymmetrically with respect to the main axis of the village.

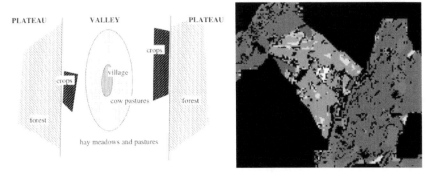

Figure 7.1. *An outline of the spatial organization of a village in Lorraine beside an excerpt from a satellite image that may correspond to it [LEB 99], [LEB 07a]. For a color version of this figure, see www.iste.co.uk/batton/geographic1.zip*

This description, in order to be used in an automatic classification process, must be translated in a formal language and related to the characteristics of the objects in the image. This issue involves qualitative spatial reasoning, a field that has seen the development of various methods based on algebras, as we will see in the following section.

7.2. Algebras used for spatial reasoning

We will describe the basic principles of spatial reasoning processes based on algebras, independently of the imperfect dimension of spatial data. After putting forward some definitions, we will describe temporal and spatial models funded on algebras, especially RCC8 (Region Connection Calculus) for topological relations. We will also present related works and mention some implementations of these models.

7.2.1. *The definition and properties of algebras, relational algebras*

DEFINITION (Boolean algebra).– *Let $(E, +, \cdot, -, 0, 1)$ be a set governed by two internal composition laws $+$ and $\cdot$ as well as a function that assigns to an element x its complement (noted $-$).*

+ and · are associative and commutative

+ and · admit a neutral element 0 and 1

+ and · are distributive in relation to each another

any element is idempotent for the two laws: $x+x = x$ and $x \cdot x = x$ and verifies:

$x + (-x) = 1$ and $x \cdot (-x) = 0$

$-(x + y) = -x \cdot -y$ and $-(x \cdot y) = -x + -y$ (De Morgan's law)

0 is absorbing for · : $\forall x, x \cdot 0 = 0$

1 is absorbing for + : $\forall x, x + 1 = 1$

EXAMPLE.– Let A be a set, then $P(A)$, i.e. the set of its parts, with the intersection (·), the union (+), and the complementary function (–), is a Boolean algebra. 0 is the empty set, 1 is the set A.

DEFINITION (binary relations).– *Given a set U, a binary relation in U is a subset of $U \times U$. The equivalence (or diagonal) relation is noted Δ, $\Delta = \{(u1, u2) \in U \times U \mid u1 = u2\}$.*

Two operations are associated with binary relations, i.e. transposition (which is used to construct the inverse relation of a relation) and composition (which is used to infer the relation between two objects based on the knowledge about the relations between each of the two objects and a third object):

– Transposition: if we consider the relation $R \subseteq U \times U$, then its transpose $R^{\smile}$ is defined by $R^{\smile} = \{(x,y) \in U \times U \mid (y,x) \in R\}$. Transposition is an involution or, in other words, $(R^{\smile})^{\smile} = R$ for any relation R.

– Composition: let R and S be two relations of $U \times U$. If $(x, y) \in R$ and $(y, z) \in S$ then $(x, z) \in R \circ S : R \circ S = \{(x, z) \in U \times U \mid (\exists y \in U)$ so that $(x, y) \in R$ and $(y, z) \in S\}$.

These two operations on relations have the following properties:

– composition is associative;

– the diagonal relation is a neutral element for composition: $\forall R, R \circ \Delta = \Delta \circ R = R$;

– transposition is distributive in relation to composition: $\forall R, \forall S, (R \circ S)^{\smile} = S^{\smile} \circ R^{\smile}$.

Now, let U be any kind of set and A be a set of binary relations in U. There is a smaller set *[A]* of binary relations closed by the Boolean operations, transposition, and composition, which contains $U \times U$, $\emptyset$, and Δ. This set of relations is a relational algebra called *the relational algebra generated* by A [TAR 41]. This algebra can be written as ($[A]$, +, $\cdot$,−, 0, 1, Δ, ⌣, ∘) where ($[A]$,+,$\cdot$,−,0,1) is a Boolean algebra.

7.2.2. *Relational algebras used for time and space*

Qualitative reasoning on time and space as a field has developed in particular in the context of constraint propagation, relying on two main sources: Allen's works [ALL 83], which define a reasoning formalism over temporal intervals, for the temporal component; and the works carried out by the Leeds school, which define the RCC8 formalism [RAN 92b], for the spatial component. In these formalisms, the algebra that includes temporal or spatial disjunctive relations plays a central role, as shown below.

Temporal algebras

We will first present a simple model, which is an algebra of points – or temporal instants [VIL 86] relying on a set of three basic relations. $B1 = \{\succ, \prec, eq\}$: $x \succ y$ means that the instant x (strictly) follows the instant y, $x \prec y$ means that x (strictly) precedes y, and x *eq* y means that the two instants are simultaneous (equal). The relations $\succ$ and $\prec$ are each other's transpose. The relation *eq* is the diagonal relation. These three basic relations result in an algebra with $2^3 = 8$ disjunctive relations, which are noted $\{\succ, \prec, eq\}$, $\{\succ, \prec\}$, $\{\succ, eq\}$, $\{\prec, eq\}$, $\{\succ\}$, $\{\prec\}$, $\{eq\}$, and $\emptyset$, respectively. For example, the notation $x \{\succ, \prec\} y$ means that the instant x precedes *or* follows the instant y. The notation $x \{\succ, \prec, eq\} y$ means that the relation between the two instants x and y is completely unknown (all relations are possible).

Finally, the two-by-two composition of the basic relations is represented in a table, illustrated in Table 7.1. For example, if two instants x and y are such that $x \prec y$ and $y \prec z$, we can deduce that $x \prec z$ (first row and first column of the table). On the other hand, if $x \prec y$ and $y \succ z$, nothing can be deduced (first row and second column of the table).

The formalism suggested by Allen [ALL 83] relies on temporal intervals and involves a set of 13 basic relations: $A = \{precedes, is\text{-}preceded\ by, meets, is\text{-}met\ by, overlaps, is\text{-}overlapped\ by, starts, is\text{-}started\ by, during,$

contains, finishes, is-finished by, equals}. The algebra generated includes 2^{13} = 8192 elements.

∘	<	>	eq
<	*{<}*	*{<, eq, >}*	*{<}*
>	*{<, eq, >}*	*{>}*	*{>}*
eq	*{<}*	*{>}*	*{eq}*

Table 7.1. *A composition table for the algebra of points – for Allen's algebra, see the presentation in [CON 07]*

Algebra for spatial relations: RCC8

The basic notion in spatial regions is the concept of part–whole relationship between two regions. This notion was formalized in a mereological context [LES 89], which then integrated the concept of connection. Thus, we refer to mereotopology. Mereotopologies are theories based on a *connection* relation (*C*), which can account for the notion of boundary. The eight relations TPP (*tangential proper part*), TPPI (*contains as TPP*, also noted as TPP-1), NTPP (*non-TPP*), NTPPI (*contains as NTPP*, also noted as NTPP-1), POs (*partially overlaps*), EC (*externally connected*), DC (*disconnected from*), and EQ (*equals*) form a set of complete and disjoint relations (only one of these relations can ever be verified between two regions, see Figure 7.2). The algebra generated, known as RCC8, includes 2^8 = 256 elements [RAN 92b].

In our example concerning image classification, we can use the RCC8 model to formalize the relationships between the various objects included in the outline illustrated in Figure 7.1. In this context, the statement "The village territory is surrounded on both sides by the state forest" can then be translated in more simple terms into EC (village-territory, state-forest$_1$), EC (village-territory, state-forest$_2$), and DC (state-forest$_1$, state-forest$_2$).

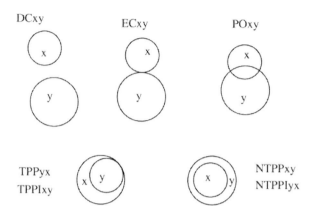

Figure 7.2. *Basic relations in RCC8*

∘	NTPP	TPP	NTPPI	TPPI	PO	EC	DC
NTPP	NTTP	NTPP	⊤	DC EC PO TPP NTPP	DC EC PO TPP NTPP	DC	DC
TPP	NTPP	TPP NTPP	DC EC PO TPPI NTPPI	DC EC PO TPP TPPI EQ	DC EC PO TPP NTPP	DC EC	DC
NTPPI	PO TPP NTPP TPPI NTPPI EQ	PO TPPI NTPPI	NTPPI	NTPPI	PO TPPI NTPPI	PO TPPI NTPPI	DC EC PO TPPI NTPPI
TPPI	PO TPP NTPP	PO TPP TPPI EQ	NTPPI	TPPI NTPPI	PO TPPI NTPPI	EC PO TPPI NTPPI	DC EC PO TPPI NTPPI
PO	PO TPP NTPP	PO TPP NTPP	DC EC PO TPPI NTPPI	DC EC PO TPPI NTPPI	⊤	DC EC PO TPPI NTPPI	DC EC PO TPPI NTPPI
EC	PO TPP NTPP	EC PO TPP NTPP	DC	DC EC	DC EC PO TPP NTPP	DC EC PO TPP TPPI EQ	DC EC PO TPPI NTPPI
DC	DC EC PO TPP NTPP	DC EC PO TPP NTPP	DC	DC	DC EC PO TPP NTPP	DC EC PO TPP NTPP	⊤

Table 7.2. *The composition table for the basic relations in RCC8*

A composition table (Table 7.2) is used for a reasoning process which is often formalized as a task that involves resolving qualitative constraints:

given a set of known relations (or constraints) between several regions (or variables), the goal is to find a scenario (i.e. a configuration of the regions) that respects these constraints. Thus, composition is used to reduce the search space. For example, Figure 7.3 represents a network of constraints with three variables, $V = \{V_1, V_2, V_3\}$, and constraints between each pair of variables (the constraint between the variables V_i and V_j is noted as $C_{i,j}$, while its inverse constraint is noted as $C_{i,j}^{-1}$): $C_{1.2}=C_{2.1}^{-1}=\{DC\}$, $C_{1.3}=C_{3.1}^{-1}=\{EC,PO\}$, $C_{3.2}=\{TPPI,EQ,PO\}$. Using the composition table, it can be seen that $\{EC,PO\} \circ \{DC\} = \{TPPI,NTPPI,DC,EC,PO\}$. Therefore, the relationship between V_3 and V_2 cannot include EQ, and finally $C_{3.2}=\{TPPI,PO\}$. A scenario that respects these constraints is presented on the right in Figure 7.3: it can be verified that V_1 POs with V_3 and is distant from V_2 which is itself a TPP of V_3.

Figure 7.3. *A network of qualitative spatial constraints and a scenario that verifies it*

Other works

While the RCC8 model for topological relations is the best known, there are also algebras for other types of spatial relations, e.g. the works carried out by Ligozat on orientation relations [LIG 98]. The works carried out by Egenhofer [EGE 89] and Egenhofer and Franzosa [EGE 92], while not in line with algebraic formalism, have established a minimum set of relations similar to the RCC8 one. The eight topological relations are seen as the result of a set of intersection operations involving the interiors (noted as x^o, y^o) and the boundaries (noted as ∂x, ∂y) of regions. For example, the relation *cover*, which corresponds to TTPI, is described by the following characteristics for two regions x and y (see Figure 7.4): non-empty intersection between the boundaries of x and y, non-empty intersections between the interiors, non-empty intersection between the interior of x and the boundary of y, and empty intersection between the boundary of x and the interior of y. This first model was expanded into the so-called nine-intersection model [EGE 93] by incorporating information about the regions' complement for regions in a discrete or continuous space (see Figure 7.5).

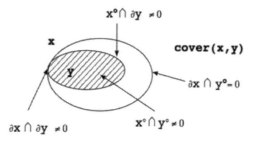

Figure 7.4. *The relation cover (x,y) – or TPPI (x,y) – as the result of the intersections between the interior and boundary parts of regions x and y*

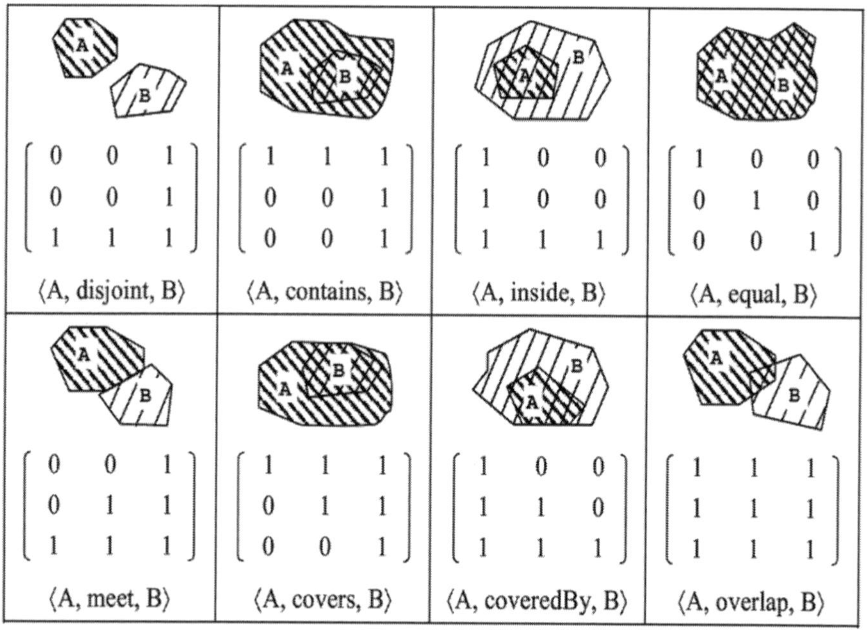

$\begin{bmatrix} 0 & 0 & 1 \\ 0 & 0 & 1 \\ 1 & 1 & 1 \end{bmatrix}$	$\begin{bmatrix} 1 & 1 & 1 \\ 0 & 0 & 1 \\ 0 & 0 & 1 \end{bmatrix}$	$\begin{bmatrix} 1 & 0 & 0 \\ 1 & 0 & 0 \\ 1 & 1 & 1 \end{bmatrix}$	$\begin{bmatrix} 1 & 0 & 0 \\ 0 & 1 & 0 \\ 0 & 0 & 1 \end{bmatrix}$
⟨A, disjoint, B⟩	⟨A, contains, B⟩	⟨A, inside, B⟩	⟨A, equal, B⟩
$\begin{bmatrix} 0 & 0 & 1 \\ 0 & 1 & 1 \\ 1 & 1 & 1 \end{bmatrix}$	$\begin{bmatrix} 1 & 1 & 1 \\ 0 & 1 & 1 \\ 0 & 0 & 1 \end{bmatrix}$	$\begin{bmatrix} 1 & 0 & 0 \\ 1 & 1 & 0 \\ 1 & 1 & 1 \end{bmatrix}$	$\begin{bmatrix} 1 & 1 & 1 \\ 1 & 1 & 1 \\ 1 & 1 & 1 \end{bmatrix}$
⟨A, meet, B⟩	⟨A, covers, B⟩	⟨A, coveredBy, B⟩	⟨A, overlap, B⟩

Figure 7.5. *The definition of topological relations as the result of nine intersections in a continuous space; the matrix includes series of rows and columns formed by the interior, boundary, and complement sets of a region: the value corresponds to the result of the intersection between the two sets [EGE 93], [PIN 11]*

Thus, this approach can verify relations based on image data. If we reconsider our example, we can then verify that each of the two objects state-forest in the image shares a boundary with the object village-territory, whereas the interiors are disjointed; that the boundaries and interiors do not overlap; and that the interiors are included in the complements (see in Figure 7.6 a simplification of the image in Figure 7.1).

Uses and implementations

Various systems have been implemented to manipulate the algebras used for spatial or temporal relations, often in an *ad hoc* manner. Some generic tools like QAT [CON 06], SparQ [WAL 06], or GQR [GAN 08] have been suggested. Let us also recall the implementations developed in classical logic languages, which benefit then from the existing reasoners: classical logics (e.g. [BEN 94], [RAN 92a]), object-based languages (e.g. [LEB 02], [MOI 07]), or, more recently, description logics (see [BEU 15], [GRU 07], [KAT 05], [ROU 13]).

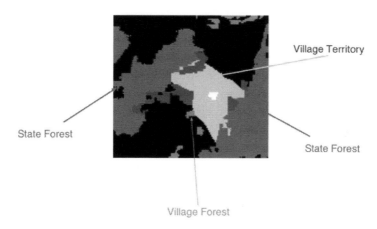

Figure 7.6. *In the simplified image, it is possible to verify the disjointed relationship each of the two state forests and the village territory, as well as the relation disjoint between the two state forests. For a color version of this figure, see www.iste.co.uk/batton/geographic1.zip*

7.3. Lattices of relation

Lattices are models that can suitably represent the algebras used for temporal or spatial relations. Due to their hierarchical structure, they can appropriately represent bodies of knowledge and the associated reasoning processes. Moreover, under certain conditions, they can establish a link between geographic information (e.g. an image showing labeled objects) and spatial knowledge. Given a Boolean algebra $(E, +, \cdot, -, 0, 1)$, the related lattice is $(E, \leq)$ where $\leq$ is a partial order relation defined by $x \leq y \leftrightarrow x \cdot y = x$. For the lattice associated with the powerset $P(A)$ of a set A, the order is given by inclusion: it can be verified for all parts x and y of $P(A)$ that "x is included in y" is equivalent to "the intersection between x and y is equal to x."

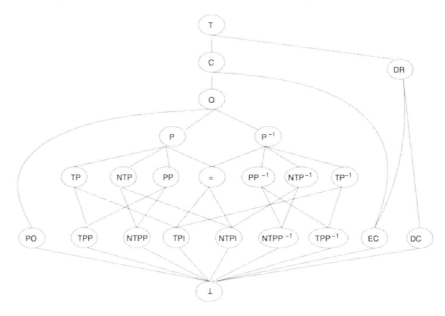

Figure 7.7. *A lattice of topological relations as defined in [RAN 92a] – the equality relation is presented as two relations noted TPI and NTPI.*

[RAN 92a] has described some lattices of topological and temporal relations. One of these lattices is represented in Figure 7.7: the most general relations are shown at the top, while the most specific ones are illustrated at the bottom (here, seven RCC8 basic relations and two equality relations depending on whether the regions have a boundary or not); the order relation is shown by the edges between the nodes that represent the relations. This lattice (automatically completed to be Boolean) may be exploited by a reasoning system. Here, the Boolean operations involved are the disjunction ($\cup$) and conjunction ($\cap$) of relations. The disjunction of two relations is obtained by following the edges of the lattice, looking for the least common super-relation (the so-called *supremum*). Thus, the disjunction of TPP and NTPP is the relation PP. The conjunction of two relations is obtained symmetrically by looking for the greatest common sub-relation (the so-called *infimum*). Thus, the conjunction of PP and TP is the relation TPP.

Specifically, an inconsistent set of relations between two regions may be easily identified: if the infimum of the relations is the empty relation (at the bottom of the lattice), then the set is inconsistent.

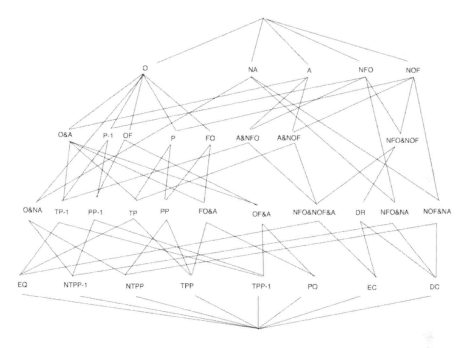

Figure 7.8. *A Galois lattice of RCC8 and primitive relations (drawn from [LEB 03]): O, A, NA, FO, NFO, OF, and NOF indicate the primitives suggested by Egenhofer [EGE 89]*

Lattices play a significant role in classifications due to their ability to manipulate various levels of information. Thus, if we consider the statement "the cultivated plots are situated between the built area and the state forest," which may be simplified as "the cultivated plots are situated on the territory of the village," we can formalize it with the proper part relation PP. If we suppose that the information calculated in the image for an object $crop_1$ is: NTTP ($crop_1$, village-territory), then the hierarchy of relations allows us to infer PP ($crop_1$, village-territory) and, therefore, to verify the consistency between the image data and the target schema.

The works carried out by [LEB 03], [NAP 07] have employed specific lattices, i.e. Galois lattices, to establish relations between operations on geographic data (such as those suggested by [EGE 89]) and RCC8 relations.

In the lattice shown in Figure 7.8, each node represents simultaneously a topological relation (e.g. TP, tangential part) and a conjunction of primitive relations between two regions x and y, which can be easily calculated in images (for TP: O, non-empty intersection of the interiors of x and y; A, non-empty intersection of the boundaries of x and y; NOF, empty intersection of the interior of x and of the boundary of y, see Figure 7.9). This lattice is merely a subset of the Boolean lattice of RCC8 relations: all the conjunctions between two relations are represented in both this lattice and the Boolean lattice (e.g. EQ = TP $\cap$ TP-1), but some disjunctions between relations are not represented.

Figure 7.9. *The relation TP (x,y) = (O $\cap$ A $\cap$ NOF) (x,y) = (TPP $\cup$ EQ) (x,y)*

7.4. Extending these models to fuzzy regions

Awareness of the uncertainty and imprecision associated with geographic information has resulted in the creation of models of objects with broad boundaries (see Chapter 5). Let us immediately point out that a broad boundary object may be modeled as a simple region inside another simple region (see Chapter 5). Thus, the RCC8 formalism and the composition table presented in Table 7.2 may be applied by considering pairs of two simple regions. Not every configuration is possible (e.g. if the boundary region of an object A is DC of the boundary region of an object B, then it will necessarily be DC of its interior).

The spatial relations between these broad boundary objects may also be established by carrying out set operations (intersection in most cases) on the various parts of the objects. Some works have tackled this question since the 1990s. We can mention in particular the works carried out by Clementini and Di Felice [CLE 97], who have extended the nine-intersection model to include broad boundary objects. Here, the interior of the regions, their boundaries (broad and noted as Δ), and their complements are considered.

This model can identify 44 relations. These relations may be seen as specialized RCC8 relations. For example, Figure 7.10 represents the various relations covered by the equality relation between simple regions: these various relations correspond to different configurations of the interior of the two regions for a common cover.

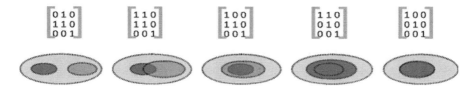

Figure 7.10. *The various relations that correspond to equality, characterized by a 3 × 3 intersection matrix for broad boundary objects. For a color version of this figure, see www.iste.co.uk/batton/geographic1.zip*

The 4×4 intersection matrix model suggested by Tang [TAN 04] considers objects with a broad boundary, which in turn presents a boundary. Calculating the relations between two objects A and B involves the intersection of eight distinct parts: the interiors of the objects (A°, B°), the interiors of their boundaries (IA°, IB°), the boundaries of the boundaries (IIA, IIB), and the complements of the objects (A⁻, B⁻). Thus, 152 relations can be identified. If we consider the example in Figure 7.11, objects A and B touch along the boundaries of their boundaries (IIA and IIB).

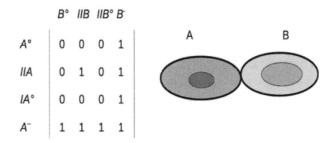

	B°	IIB	IIB°	B⁻
A°	0	0	0	1
IIA	0	1	0	1
IA°	0	0	0	1
A⁻	1	1	1	1

Figure 7.11. *A relation between two broad boundary objects whose boundaries, in turn, have a boundary and its description in a 4 × 4 intersection matrix as defined by [TAN 04]. For a color version of this figure, see www.iste.co.uk/batton/geographic1.zip*

These sets of disjoint binary relations can generate algebras that enable the same reasoning processes used for simple spatial objects. However, it should be noted that the complexity of reasoning processes grows according to the number of relations. This type of approach has been used to identify objects in satellite images. Tang applied it to the identification of a change in land cover [TAN 04].

Let us reconsider the example which we have focused on throughout this chapter. If we reconsider the original image (Figure 7.1), we can see that it has not been possible to assign certain pixels (in black) to some objects. This makes it trickier to calculate a fine boundary and relations that rely on the intersection between boundaries. An option would be to force the attribution of these pixels to neighboring objects. This is the process carried out on the image in Figure 7.6. Another option implies considering broad boundaries, so that it is possible to take into account the uncertainty related to the data (here, for example, the fact that an unassigned pixel may belong to both the boundary of the object state-forest and the boundary of the object village-territory).

Besides the models presented earlier, some works have been carried out on fuzzy representations of other spatial relations, such as orientation and distance relations or the "between" ternary relation (see e.g. [BLO 05], [HUD 08]), in order to consider the uncertainty related to both data and the various terms used by experts to describe the structures to identify.

7.5. References

[ALL 83] ALLEN J.F., "Maintaining knowledge about temporal intervals", *Communications of the ACM*, vol. 26, no. 11, pp. 832–843, 1983.

[BAC 04] BACHACOU J., LE BER F., MANGELINCK L., "Analyse des paysages agricoles: définition d'indicateurs pour la reconnaissance de structures spatiales sur images satellitaires", in MONESTIEZ P., LARDON S., SEGUIN B. (eds), *Organisation spatiale des activités agricoles et processus environnementaux*, INRA Éditions, Paris, pp. 279–302, 2004.

[BEN 94] BENNETT B., "Spatial reasoning with propositional logics", in *Fourth International Conference on Principles of Knowledge Representation and Reasoning*, Bonn, Germany, pp. 51–62, May 1994.

[BEU 15] DE BERTRAND DE BEUVRON F., MARC-ZWECKER S., ZANNI-MERK C. *et al.*, "Combining ontological and qualitative spatial reasoning: application to urban images interpretation", in *Fifth International Joint Conference, IC3K*, Vilamoura, Portugal, September 2013. Revised selected papers, Springer CCIS vol. 454, pp. 182–198, 2015.

[BLO 05] BLOCH I., "Fuzzy spatial relationships for image processing and interpretation: a review", *Image and Vision Computing*, vol. 23, no. 2, pp. 89–110, 2005.

[CLE 97] CLEMENTINI E., DI FELICE P., "Approximate topological relations", *International Journal of Approximate Reasoning*, vol. 16, no. 2, pp. 173–204, 1997.

[CON 06] CONDOTTA J.-F., LIGOZAT G., SAADE M., "A generic toolkit for n-ary qualitative temporal and spatial calculi", in *Thirteenth International Symposium on Temporal Representation and Reasoning (TIME'06)*, Budapest, Hungary, pp. 78–86, 2006.

[CON 07] CONDOTTA J.-F., WÜRBEL E., "Réseaux de contraintes temporelles et spatiales", in LE BER F., LIGOZAT G., PAPINI O. (eds), *Raisonnements sur l'espace et le temps: des modèles aux applications*, Hermès-Lavoisier, Paris, pp. 181–223, 2007.

[EGE 89] EGENHOFER M.J., "A formal definition of binary topological relationships", in *Foundations of Data Organization and Algorithms (FODO 1989)*, LNCS, Paris, France, vol. 367, pp. 457–472, 1989.

[EGE 92] EGENHOFER M.J., FRANSOZA R., "Point-set topological spatial relations", *International Journal of Geographical Information Systems*, vol. 5, no. 2, pp. 161–174, 1992.

[EGE 93] EGENHOFER M.J., SHARMA J., "Topological relations between regions in R2 and Z2", in *Advances in Spatial Data, Third International Symposium (SSD'93)*, LNCS, Singapore, vol. 692, pp. 316–336, June 1993.

[GAN 08] GANTNER Z., WESTPHAL M., WÖLFL S., "GQR-A fast reasoner for binary qualitative constraint calculi", in *AAAI'08 Workshop on Spatial and Temporal Reasoning*, Chicago, IL, USA, 2008.

[GRU 07] GRÜTTER R., BAUER-MESSMER B., "Combining OWL with RCC for spatioterminological reasoning on environmental data", in *Third International Workshop on OWL: Experiences and Directions*, Innsbruck, Austria, June 2007.

[HUD 08] HUDELOT C., ATIF J., BLOCH I., "Fuzzy spatial relation ontology for image interpretation", *Fuzzy Sets and Systems*, vol. 159, no. 15, pp. 1929–1951, 2008.

[KAT 05] KATZ Y., GRAU B.C., "Representing qualitative spatial information in OWL-DL", in *Proceedings of OWL: Experiences and Directions*, Galway, Ireland, 2005.

[LEB 99] LE BER F., MANGELINCK L., NAPOLI A., "Représentation de relations et classification de structures spatiales", *Revue d'Intelligence Artificielle*, vol. 13, no. 2, pp. 441–467, 1999.

[LEB 02] LE BER F., NAPOLI A., "The design of an object-based system for representing and classifying spatial structures and relations", *Journal of Universal Computer Science*, vol. 8, no. 8, pp. 751–773, 2002.

[LEB 03] LE BER F., NAPOLI A., "Design and comparison of lattices of topological relations for spatial representation and reasoning", *Journal of Experimental and Theoretical Artificial Intelligence*, vol. 15, no. 3, pp. 331–371, 2003.

[LEB 07a] LE BER F., "Reconnaissance de paysages agricoles à l'aide de treillis de relations", in LE BER F., LIGOZAT G., PAPINI O. (eds), *Raisonnements sur l'espace et le temps: des modèles aux applications*, Hermès-Lavoisier, Paris, pp. 291–304, 2007.

[LEB 07b] LE BER F., LIGOZAT G., PAPINI O. (eds), *Raisonnements sur l'espace et le temps: des modèles aux applications*, Hermès-Lavoisier, Paris, 2007.

[LES 89] LESNIEWSKI S., *Sur les fondements de la mathématique*, translated from Polish (1927–1931), Hermès, Paris, 1989.

[LIG 98] LIGOZAT G., "Reasoning about cardinal directions", *Journal of Visual Languages and Computing*, vol. 1, no. 9, pp. 23–44, 1998.

[MOI 07] MOISUC B., CAPPONI C., GENOUD P. *et al.*, "Modélisation algébrique et représentation de connaissances par objets en AROM", *Langages et Modèles à Objets*, Toulouse, France, 2007.

[NAP 07] NAPOLI A., LE BER F., "The Galois lattice as a hierarchical structure for topological relations", *Annals of Mathematics and Artificial Intelligence*, vol. 49, nos 1–4, pp. 1–20, 2007.

[PIN 11] PINET F., DUBOISSET M., SCHNEIDER M., "Modelling spatial integrity constraints with OCL", *Revue Internationale de Géomatique*, vol. 21, pp. 95–123, 2011.

[RAN 92a] RANDELL D.A., COHN A.G., "Exploiting lattices in a theory of space and time", *Computers and Mathematics with Applications*, vol. 23, nos 6–9, pp. 459–476, 1992.

[RAN 92b] RANDELL D.A., CUI Z., COHN A.G., "A spatial logic based on regions and connection", in *Third International Conference on Principles of Knowledge Representation and Reasoning* (KR'92), pp. 165–176, 1992.

[ROU 13] ROUSSEY C., PINET F., SCHNEIDER M., "Representations of topological relations between simple regions in description logics: from formalization to consistency checking", *International Journal of Agricultural and Environmental Information Systems*, vol. 4, no. 2, pp. 50–69, 2013.

[TAN 04] TANG X., Spatial object modeling in fuzzy topological spaces: with applications to land cover change, PhD thesis, University of Twente, Enschede, The Netherlands, 2004.

[TAR 41] TARSKI A., "On the calculus of relations", *Journal of Symbolic Logic*, vol. 6, no. 3, pp. 73–89, 1941.

[VIL 86] VILAIN M., KAUTZ H., "Constraint propagation algorithms for temporal reasoning", in *Fifth National Conference on Artificial Intelligence (AAAI'86)*, pp. 377–382, 1986.

[WAL 06] WALLGRÜN J.O., FROMMBERGER L., WOLTER D. *et al.*, "Qualitative spatial representation and reasoning in the SparQ-Toolbox", in *International Conference on Spatial Cognition*, LNCS, Bremen, Germany, vol. 4387, pp. 39–58, September 2006.

Reasoning in Modal Logic
for Uncertain Data

8.1. Introduction

In this section, our goal is to study some possibilities so as to deduce new information based on uncertain knowledge. We will present the semantic of modal operators and their use to reason about uncertain data. Here, uncertainty is considered in relation to the qualitative aspect of the reality observed rather than from a quantitative perspective. We will explain the general reasoning principles behind first-order predicate calculus before applying them to modal systems.

To illustrate the various reasoning processes tackled in this chapter, we will use an example based on some data stored in the SIGEMO system (*Système d'Information sur la Gestion des Épandages de Matières Organiques*, or "Computerized System for the Management of the Spreading of Organic Matters"). SIGEMO has been developed to monitor the practices involved in the spreading of organic matters in France [SOU 06]. Its goal is to process, assess, and monitor spreading plans. The variety of the actors involved in this project is significant: the producers of spreadable matter (local authorities, manufacturers, livestock farmers, etc.), the research units that prepare the spreading plans for the producers, the institutions (the Ministry of Health, Agriculture, Infrastructure) that examine the cases, and the independent bodies that assess the spreading plans. To determine which products can be spread on French soil, the land has been divided into areas, parcels, and zones. A spread area is a set of spread parcels. Based on the area

Chapter written by Élisabeth GAVIGNET and Nadine CULLOT.

in question, a limited number of products are allowed. Each parcel, in turn, includes appropriate zones on which the products are spread. The parcels and zones are defined by geographic data. The files about the spreading plans record the quantities of products to spread, the matters to spread, the zones to treat, and the agricultural parcels in question. This system significantly needs to work with reliable data in order to be effective. In particular, in this field, there are strict rules that determine constraints which may be exploited to detect anomalies. Knowing which matters will be spread and which zones should be treated reveals whether the spreading plan is valid or not. On the other hand, if data are imperfect, and if it turns out that the geographic information about the zone in question reveals that the area straddles a natural zone which should receive no spreadable product, this anomaly must be reported. This also applies when a product expected to be used is not allowed in this zone. However, before being able to report these anomalies, it is necessary to translate these constraints into a formal language which supports logical reasoning processes.

8.2. Reasoning in first-order predicate calculus

First-order predicate calculus is commonly used to make deductions based on knowledge represented by formulae by using the Robinson resolution principle [KOW 74, ROB 65]. The language of first-order predicate calculus is defined thanks to a set of predicate symbols, a set of function symbols, a set of variables, and a set of logical connectives. A number of arguments (arity) are assigned to each function and predicate symbol. Constants are functions with arity equal to 0. In the rest of the chapter, variables will be denoted by capital letters (P, S, etc.) and constants in lower case (as1, ap1, moc, etc.), so that readers will be able to clearly distinguish between the symbols used in this language.

Thanks to the elements of the predicate logic language, it is possible not only to express that some statements are true – "bb is mud that derives from the sewage treatment plant B" – but also to express some statements that can explain logical consequences: "if b is mud, then b is a spreadable product". These two examples illustrate, on the one hand, a fact, and on the other hand, a **rule** expressed as a Horn clause, which is a conjunction of terms, noted $P_1, ..., P_n \rightarrow P$ where P and P_i are predicates. The right side of a Horn clause includes at most one predicate. A **fact** is a predicate without a variable. Rules will make it possible to look for information so that eventually new facts can be deduced.

Let us reconsider the example concerning product spreading with a very specific case described in the image below (Figure 8.1). This real case will lay the foundations for an explanation of how it is possible to reason with a system based on predicate logic. Several pieces of information found in this image should be kept in mind:

– it represents two parcels, ap1 and ap2, on which products are allowed to be spread;

– one of them, ap1, is divided into two appropriate zones, as1 and as2;

– the image clearly mentions spreadable products and their source (mud produced by a sewage-treatment plant, organic matter produced by a farm);

– in zone as1, the mud produced by the sewage-treatment plants A and B and the organic matter produced by the farm C are authorized;

– in zone as2, only the organic matter produced by farm C is allowed to be spread.

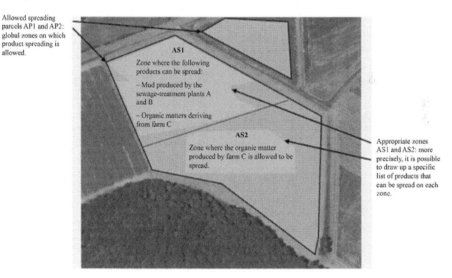

Figure 8.1. *An illustrative case study [DUB 07]*

This example includes objects (products, parcels, appropriate zones) and relations between these objects (a zone is in a parcel, a product derives from somewhere). Various predicates will be required to represent these objects and relations:

– the predicate **mud(B, S)** represents the fact that the substance defined by the variable "B" is mud produced by the source (the sewage-treatment plant) defined by "S";

– similarly, the predicate **matOrga(M, S)** represents the fact that the substance defined by the variable "M" is some organic matter produced by the source (the farm) defined by the variable "S";

– the predicate **product(P)** refers to the fact that the product defined by the variable "P" is a spreadable product;

– the predicate **is_in(Z, PA)** represents the fact that the appropriate zone "Z" is situated in the parcel defined by the variable "PA";

– similarly, the predicate **spread_on(P, Z)** means that the product defined by the variable "P" has been spread on the zone defined by the variable "Z";

– finally, the predicate **spreading_authorized(P, Z)** refers to the fact that the product defined by the variable "P" can be spread on the zone "Z".

To partially represent the knowledge involved in the example illustrated by Figure 8.1, some facts that correspond to the situation described will be defined.

Fact to translate	Translation into predicate logic
Zone "as1" is in parcel "ap2"	is_in(as1, ap2)
The substance referred to as "moc" corresponds to organic matter that derives from the farm "c"	matOrga(moc, c)
The substance defines as "bb" refers to mud that derives from the sewage-treatment plant "b"	mud(bb, b)
The organic matter "moc" has been spread on zone "as1"	spread_on(moc, as1)
The organic matter "moc" can be spread on zone "as1"	spreading_authorized(moc, as1)

Table 8.1. *Sample facts about spreading*

To keep considering the products spread, it is possible to state that a spreadable product is either mud or organic matter. Two rules are required for this:

mud(b, s) → product(b)

matOrga(m, s) → product(m).

Similarly, using a rule makes it possible to discover some anomalies based on products that have already been spread. For example, while examining the set of products spread on a zone, one may question the legitimacy of the new facts, and, by making comparisons with the officially authorized products, the infractions can be discovered. The following rule shows that if "P" is a spreadable product that has been spread on a zone "Z" belonging to the parcel "PA", then it is detected that this product "P" has been spread on the parcel "PA":

product(P), spread_on(P, Z), is_in(Z, PA) → detected_spreading(P, PA).

This type of formula can be used to retrieve all the products spread on the parcels. It is better to present the unification and substitution processes beforehand, and then to specify the deductive process.

The variable substitution σ is a function that assigns terms to variables. It involves replacing in a formula all the identifiable variables mentioned in σ with the substitution value.

– Let σ be a substitution with $\sigma = \{P/moc\}$ and formula F1: product(P). Applying the substitution σ to the formula F1, denoted $\sigma(F1)$, yields $\sigma(F1) = $ product(moc).

Two formulae are said to be unifiable if there is a series of substitutions that make the two formulae equal, roughly the same as when the variables are renamed.

– Assuming there are two formulae F2 = spread_on(moc, PA) and F3 = spread_on(P, as1), to unify them, it is necessary to find θ such that $\theta(F2) = \theta(F3)$. This can be done thanks to $\theta = \{P/moc, PA/as1\}$. In fact, $\theta(F2) = $ spread_on(moc, as1), and the same can be obtained by replacing P with moc in F3.

In predicate logic, to prove that a formula G is satisfiable (true) in a set $\mathcal{F}$ of formulae $\{H_1, \ldots, H_n\}$, we will proceed by refuting and implementing the variant of the Robinson resolution method [ROB 65]. This method involves demonstrating the inconsistency of a set of formulae. Let G be a formula. To show that G is a logical consequence of the set of formulae $\mathcal{F}$, it is necessary to try to refute $\mathcal{F} \cup \{G\}$.

$\mathcal{F} \models G$ if and only if $(\mathcal{F} \cup \{\neg G\})$ is inconsistent.

In practice, this proof-by-refutation technique is applied iteratively according to the following principle:

– $\mathcal{F}_0 = \mathcal{F} \cup \{\neg G_0\}$, where G_0 is the goal at the beginning of the resolution.

The series $\mathcal{F}_1, \mathcal{F}_2, \ldots$ is calculated according to the following process:

– $\mathcal{F}_i = \mathcal{F} \cup \{\neg G_i\}$, where $\neg G_i$ is the sub-goal obtained as the resolvent formula of $\neg G_{i-1}$ and of formula H_j for $j \in [1,n]$, of $\mathcal{F}$.

The process is over when the empty formula is deduced. The differentiation of the empty formula $\varnothing$ based on $\mathcal{F}_0$ is said to be a refutation of $\mathcal{F}_0$. Otherwise, the set $\mathcal{F}_0$ is satisfiable; therefore, G is unsatisfiable in $\mathcal{F}$.

The variant of the Robinson resolution employed is the SLD-resolution (Selective Linear Definite). This is a linear input resolution method, which turns out to be complete when applied to an inconsistent set of Horn clauses.

We will apply this method to the data provided in the example of spreadable products in order to illustrate how it works. The set $\mathcal{F}$ includes all the aforementioned facts and rules, which are shown again in Table 8.2. The goal, denoted G, is the set of spreadable products: $G = \{product(P)\}$

$\mathcal{F}_0 = \mathcal{F} \cup \{\neg product(P)\} = \{H_1, H_2, H_3, H_4, H_5, H_6, H_7, H_8, \neg product(P)\}$.

$\mathcal{F}_1 = \mathcal{F} \cup \{\neg mud(P, S)\} = \{H_1, H_2, H_3, H_4, H_5, H_6, H_7, H_8, \neg mud(P, S)\}$ obtained by adding the resolvent formula of $\neg product(P)$ and H_6 ($mud(B, S) \rightarrow product(B)$).

$\mathcal{F}_2 = \mathcal{F} \cup \{\neg\text{mud(bb, b)}\} = \{H_1, H_2, H_3, H_4, H_5, H_6, H_7, H_8, \neg\text{mud(bb,}$
b)\}$ by adding the resolvent formula of $\neg$ mud(P, S) and H_3, with the substitution $\{\text{P/bb, S/b}\}$.

Fact and rules of the set $\mathcal{F}$	Ref
is_in(as1, ap2)	H_1
matOrga(moc, c)	H_2
mud(bb, b)	H_3
spread_on(moc, as1)	H_4
spreading_authorized(moc, as1)	H_5
mud(B, S) → product(B)	H_6
matOrga(M, S) → product(M)	H_7
product(P), spread_on(P, Z), is_in(Z, PA) → detected_spreading (P, PA)	H_8

Table 8.2. *The set of formulae for spreading*

The simultaneous existence of $\neg$mud(bb, b) and its inverse H_3 (mud(bb, b)) makes it possible to deduce an empty clause, thus ending the resolution. The result of this resolution shows that the goal product(P) is satisfiable in $\mathcal{F}$ and one of the values that satisfy this goal is "bb". The series of resolutions of these unification operations may be outlined in a resolution tree (Figure 8.2). The leaves represent the formulae of the set $\mathcal{F}$. Each node is the resolvent of the formulae located on the branches of the node. The substitutions that have made it possible to unify the formulae are located on one of the branches.

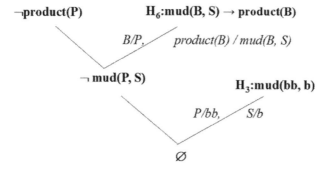

Figure 8.2. *A solution tree for the goal product(P)*

Another solution (Figure 8.3), i.e. "moc", could have been found by choosing during stage 1 the resolvent of the formula H₇ with ¬G instead of the resolvent of the formula H₆ with ¬G. Solving the goal ¬product(P) implies solving the sub-goal ¬matOrga(P, S) which, by unifying with the formula H₂ (matOrga(moc, c)), adds the new formula ¬matOrga(moc, c). This fact and its negation result in the empty formula. Thus, the goal product(P) has another value that satisfies it.

The reasoning processes examined in this section exploit only data without uncertainty. The rest of this chapter will illustrate how these mechanisms can be applied to uncertain data.

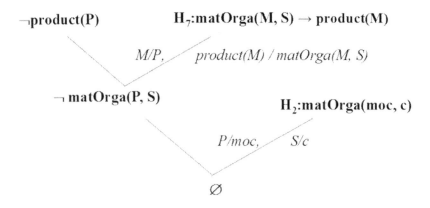

Figure 8.3. *Another solution tree for the goal product(P)*

8.3. Reasoning in modal logic

Modal logic is a type of logic that is supplemented by modal operators that can nuance the representation of reality [GAV 15, GAV 16]. These new operators allow a user to be able to express a doubt or uncertainty about the veracity of the information he or she provides.

In the context considered as an example, i.e. spreading products on parcels, uses may be of different kinds. They may, among other things, be derived from uncertainties about the observable elements and lead the user (an expert in his or her field) to make hypotheses and put forward facts that are not necessarily true. These facts may encourage the expert to think that there is some doubt about the origin of some spreadable products. How can he or she represent this uncertainty so that it will be considered in reasoning processes?

The new necessary (□) and possible (◊) operators can be used to represent this distinction. Thus, if F is a fact, respectively a rule, □F can be read as "F is necessarily true", "F is always true", "F is compulsory", and "F is true everywhere". Conversely, its dual ◊ F (¬□¬ F) can be interpreted as "it is possible that F", "F is sometimes true", "F is allowed", "F is true somewhere".

Therefore, to express uncertainty about the nature of a spreadable product or the fact that a product may have been spread on a zone, we will write the following:

– ◊ mud(ba, a), if we mean that the substance "ba" may be mud that derives from the source "a";

– ◊ spread_on(mob, as2), to report that the product "mob" may have been spread on zone "as2."

Conversely, this is what we will write to show that we have no doubt about the nature of a product or the presence of a zone in a parcel:

– □ matOrga(mob, b), to state that "mob" is definitely organic matter that derives from "b".

– □ is_in (as2, ap1), to express that the appropriate zone "as2" is necessarily situated in the parcel "ap1".

It is also possible to express impossibility. In fact, stating that F is impossible means stating that it is not possible to obtain any true F, which entails the fact that F is necessarily false (□ ¬F).

Initially, based on a set of facts that may or may not include these modalities, it becomes possible to proceed to interrogate the fact base.

Let us suppose that the following set of facts is available (see Table 8.3).

Facts with or without modality	Ref
spread_on(moc, as1)	f01
is_in(as1, ap1)	f02
matOrga(moc, c)	f03
☐ spread_on(ba, as1)	☐ f04
☐ is_in(as2, ap1)	☐ f05
◊ spread_on(mob, as2)	◊ f06
☐ matOrga(mob, b)	☐ f07
◊ mud(ba, a)	◊ f08
☐ mud(bb, b)	☐ f09

Table 8.3. *Facts related to the spreadable products*

This set of facts does not necessarily represent a reality but, rather, an interplay of tests that provide a variety of situations so as to illustrate the reasoning processes. In the rest of this chapter, each fact has been numbered f*i* (f for fact and *i* an integer in two positions) for ease of reference.

According to what has been written about the usefulness of SIGEMO, at any time, an organization may want to ensure that the spreading constraints required on a zonal level have been respected. In order to verify this, the issue is first to find out which products have been spread on each zone, if the goal is verification on a global level, or on a specific zone for a limited verification, and then to compare this list to that of the authorized products.

In the example presented in Figure 8.1, it is pointed out that only the organic matters that derive from farm C, such as "moc", are authorized in the appropriate zone, "as2". The set of facts mentioned in Table 8.3 indicates that the product "mob" (organic matter produced from farm B) may have been spread on the parcel "as2" (◊ f06). However, "mob" derives from farm B instead of farm C, and, according to the elements presented in Figure 8.1, this product has not been authorized in the zone "as2". During verification, this anomaly needs to be reported. To retrieve the products that may have been spread on a given zone, it is necessary to solve the goal ◊ spread_on (P, Z), where P represents the products and Z represents the zones where the products have been spread.

It is necessary to improve semantic descriptions slightly more if the goal is to take into account that a formula may be necessary or possible. The one that is generally used is Kripke's description, which assesses a formula not for a world (the real world) but for a set of worlds. This is the so-called possible world theory, which considers the existence of parallel worlds that can gain access to one another. A world remains characterized by formulae which are true or false. This world sees only the worlds to which it can gain access. An interpretation gives, for each rule, the worlds where it is interpreted as true.

Considering the example of spreadable products, focusing on the facts □f05 and ◊f06 can illustrate the possible world theory. These facts derive from two worlds: in the first world f05 and f06 are true, whereas in the second world, only f05 is true. The representation of these worlds can be seen in Figure 8.4, where the arrows represent the possibility of each world gaining access to others. The fact f05 is necessarily true in the world w as it is true in all its accessible worlds (u and v). Conversely, as the fact f6 is only true in one of them (v), it becomes an uncertain fact in w. The world w includes a view of reality based on the information present in the worlds u and v.

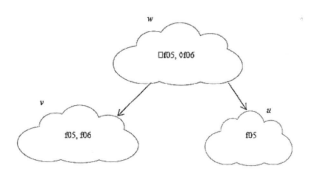

Figure 8.4. *A representation of the worlds*

On a general level, the formula □ F is true in a world w if F is true in all the worlds that are accessible from w. On the contrary, the formula ◊ F is true in a world w if F is true in at least one world that can be accessed from w.

The possible world theory involves a certain number of axioms, including the basic axiom, denoted K. Other axioms may be added to the basic system to create other systems. The axioms used in deductions are illustrated in the following paragraph.

K: □ (P → Q) → (□ P → □ Q): Kripke's axiom, which considers the distributivity of the modal operator. If necessarily (P implies Q), then P, necessarily true, implies that Q is also necessarily true. If, in all the worlds, Q can be deduced from P, then from necessarily P it will be possible to deduce necessarily Q.

– N: P → □ P: the necessitation inference axiom infers that what is true in the real world is necessarily true in all worlds.

– T: □ P → P: this axiom states that what is necessarily true in all worlds is true in the real world.

– D: □ P → ◊ P: this axiom states that if P is necessarily true in all worlds, it is possibly true in at least one of them.

– B: P → □ ◊ P: this axiom states that if P is true in the real world, it is necessarily true in at least one world.

– 4: □ P→ □ □ P: this axiom states if we necessarily have P, we can infer that P will also be necessarily true in all worlds.

– 5: ◊ P→ □ ◊ P: this axiom states that if P is possibly true, then it will be also possibly true in all worlds.

Taking into account the previous axioms, several modal logic systems can be built. The name of each system is generally the series of letters that identify the axioms. The system K includes the axioms K and N. The system KD corresponds to the system K completed by the axiom D. Some abbreviations are also used, for example S4 for the system that corresponds to the axioms KT4.

After providing these theoretical elements, we will reconsider our problem and show how it is possible to find out all the products that may have been spread on the various zones. Solving the formula ◊ spread_on(P, Z) yields the three following solutions:

– (mob, as2): first, unifying the goal ◊ spread_on(P, Z) with the fact ◊f06 (◊ spread_on(mob, as2)) reveals that some organic matter "mob" that derives from the farm B has potentially been spread on the zone "as2". This first result can already identify one of the products spread on the zone "as2".

– (ba, as1): solving the same goal ◊ spread_on(P, Z), but this time, taking into consideration the axiom D, we find out that "ba" is a product spread on the zone "as1". In fact, unifying ☐ f04 and the axiom D makes it possible to deduce a new fact ◊f04 (◊ spread_on(ba, as1)) which, when unified with ◊ spread_on(P, Z), yields the pair (ba, as1) as another solution.

– (moc, as1): this last result can be obtained by taking into consideration the fact f01. This becomes possible when the axiom N (P → ☐ P) is added to the system D. Thanks to the two axioms D and N, the system deduces another pair (moc, as1) that validates the goal ◊ spread_on(P, Z). Applying the axiom N to the fact (spread-on(moc, as1)) can generate a new fact (☐ spread_on(moc, as1)) which, as a result unified with the goal, yields the last solution (moc, as1).

When the solver is interrogated about the products that may have been spread on the various zones, it only takes into consideration "possibly true" data. To force it to extend its search to all the worlds (formulae that are "necessarily true" everywhere), or even all the data provided regardless of its uncertainty, the axioms D (☐ P → ◊ P) and N (P → ☐ P) must be included in the modal logic system.

Axioms used	Results (product, zone)
K	(mob, as2)
D	(mob, as2) + (ba, as1)
D + N	(mob, as2) + (ba, as1) + (mob, as1)

Table 8.4. *Results obtained by solving the goal ◊ spread_on(P, Z)*

Table 8.4 summarizes the values of the pairs found by the solver when solving the formula ◊ spread_on(P, Z) and highlights the difference between the responses according to the axioms considered in the reasoning process. Based on the expected results, a user may choose which axioms to use. Thus, employing the axiom N, as is the case in the example, indicates that it is possible to reason simultaneously on facts with or without modality. In our example, the facts ◊f06, ☐f04, and f01 have been exploited. The first two use modalities, whereas the last one has no modality and yet made it possible to discover a product that had been spread.

This first part used only facts defined by users and axioms that can deduce new facts, especially when looking for anomalies. The advantage of this type of interrogation may seem limited when the number of facts is as low as the one suggested, but it may become crucial very quickly when data are significant. This is systematically the case when the issue is to collect information that derives from several sources. We should now keep focusing on the use of modalities by implementing the rules that are specific to the field. Three rules have already been provided at the beginning of this chapter. They will be denoted in the rest of the chapter as the letter r and a number. A spreadable product can be either mud or organic matter (rules r1 and r2). If a product has been spread on a zone situated in a parcel, then it is detected as spread in the parcel (rule r3). These rules are assumed to be true in any case. They are grouped in Table 8.5.

Rules of the field	Ref
$\Box$ (mud(B, S) $\rightarrow$ product(B))	$\Box$r1
$\Box$ (matOrga(M, S) $\rightarrow$ product(M))	$\Box$r2
$\Box$ (product(P), spread_on(P, Z), is_in(Z, PA) $\rightarrow$ detected_spreading(P, PA))	$\Box$r3

Table 8.5. *Rules of the field*

To illustrate the role of these systems in the example of the products spread, we will simultaneously employ the axiom K, which is crucial for rule processing; the axiom D, to extend the reasoning process not only to the possible formulae but also to the formulae that are necessarily true; and finally the axiom N to indiscriminately process the formulae described with the modality "necessary" or without any modality at all. Thus, we will obtain as much information as possible about the products spread on the parcels. We will also refer to axioms and theorems that may be derived from K and N, that is:

axioms: $(P \rightarrow Q) \rightarrow (\Box P \rightarrow \Box Q)$ and $(P \rightarrow Q) \rightarrow (\Diamond P \rightarrow \Diamond Q)$,

theorems: $\Box (P \wedge Q) \rightarrow (\Box P \wedge \Box Q)$ and $(\Box P \wedge \Box Q) \rightarrow \Box (P \wedge Q)$.

To obtain all the products spread on the parcels in the example, it is advisable to solve the goal $\Box$ detected_spreading(P, PA) with the facts summarized in Table 8.3 and the rule $\Box$ r3 in the system KD (K, D, N).

Applying the distributive rule stated in the axiom K to □ r3 means that solving □ detected_spreading(P, PA) is the same as finding the solutions of the formula □ (product(P) ∧ spread_on(P, Z) ∧ is_in(Z, PA)). Applying one of the derived theorems (□ (P ∧ Q) → (□P ∧ □Q)) allows us to obtain a new formula to solve which is the conjunction of the following formulae:

□ product(P) ∧ □ spread_on(P, Z) ∧ □ is_in(Z, PA).

– By unifying the first predicate of this formula with the rule □r1 and then with the rule □r2, three products satisfy □ product(P): "moc" for the existence of the fact f03 (matOrga(moc, c)), "mob" for the fact □ f07 (□matOrga(mob, b)) and "bb" for the fact □ f09 (□mud(bb, b)).

– Solving the following predicate □ spread_on(P, Z) removes from the previous result the values "bb" and "mob", leaving only the pair (moc, as1) as a result.

– The last part of the solution involves solving □ is_in(as1, PA). This can be done with the fact f02 (is_in(as1, ap2)). The spread product detected is "moc", i.e. organic matter that derives from the farm C, on the parcel "ap2". This is indeed normal, if we take into consideration the constraints created by the context, and natural, given that the solving process has only relied on facts that were necessarily true.

To consider uncertain facts, i.e. those indicated by the possible modality (◊), such as ◊f06 (◊spread_on(mob, as2)) and ◊f08 (◊mud(ba, a)), it is necessary to focus on the search for products which have "possibly" been spread on the parcels. In other words, it is necessary to look for the pairs that verify ◊ detected_spreading(P, PA). The solving process involves three phases: looking among all the uncertain facts, then using the axiom D (□ P → ◊ P) to look among all the facts that are necessarily true since they are possible facts, and finally using the axiom N (P → □ P) to look for all the other facts (those without modality).

– In the end, after solving □ detected_spreading(P, PA), the solver finds a supplementary product, i.e. the mud "ba", due to the fact ◊f08 while solving ◊ product(P).

– In the following stage, two zones ("as1" and "as2") will be chosen since products have been spread on them (unification with f01 for "moc", with □ f04 for "ba", and with ◊ f06 for "mob").

– The last solving stage will reproduce the parcel "ap1" since, in the example, the two zones are part of the same parcel (is_in (as1, ap1) and ☐ is_in(as2, ap1)).

Given the results obtained (Table 8.6) and in comparison with the products that have actually been authorized, it can be easily seen that an unauthorized product ("mob": organic matter that derives from farm B) has been spread on the parcel "ap1", which should only receive organic matter deriving from farm C. Besides, since "ba" is a product that is not guaranteed to be mud deriving from farm A (◊ mud(ba, a)), the fact that it is spread on the zone "as1" (☐ spread_o (ba, as1)), while necessarily true, leads the solver to deduce uncertainty about its authorization in the parcel. These deductions, certain or uncertain, are very significant and may provide valuable help when looking for inconsistency.

Axioms	Results obtained for ◊ detected_spreading(P, PA)
K + D + N	(moc, ap1), (ba, ap1), (mob, ap1)
K + D	(mob, ap1)
K	No result

Table 8.6. *Results of ◊ detected_spreading(P, PA) with different axioms*

These two examples of deduction, the former only involving facts and the second using a rule, illustrate in part the advantage offered by reasoning in modal logic. With such a system of axioms, it is possible to distinguish accurately between what is certain and what is not.

Most research on the representation of uncertainty in geomatics focuses on the quantitative aspect, but it is also possible to represent the qualitative aspect. When dealing with large amounts of data, the ability to assess the quality of the information stored is fundamental. Modal logic programming should be seen as a complement to other representations of uncertainty. It can provide simulations that may constitute suitable tools for an expert to assess the plausibility of the hypotheses made. Using this type of representation may also turn out to be very useful when knowledge is supplied by various individuals and the quantity of information is such that a human being can no longer monitor his or her global consistency. Any reader who is interested in the topic can find other works such as semantics tables or sequent calculus, which are examined in depth in [LEB 07].

8.4. References

[DUB 07] DUBOISSET M., Un système de contraintes d'intégrité OCL pour les bases de données spatiales – application à un système d'information pour l'épandage agricole, Thesis, Université Blaise Pascal, Clermont-Ferrand, 2007.

[GAV 15] GAVIGNET É., LECLERCQ E., CULLOT N. *et al.*, "De l'usage des logiques modales pour la gestion de l'incertitude des données : application en archéologie", *11th International Conference Spatial Analysis and GEOmatics (SAGEO2015)*, Hammamet, Tunisia, pp 164–178, November 2015.

[GAV 16] GAVIGNET É., LECLERCQ É., CULLOT N. *et al.*, "Raisonner en logique modale sur l'incertitude liée aux données – application en archéologie", *Revue Internationale de Géomatique*, vol. 26, no. 4, pp. 467–490, 2016.

[KOW 74] KOWALSKI R., "Predicate logic as programming language", *IFIP Congress*, Stockholm, Sweden, vol. 74, pp. 544–569, 1974.

[LEB 07] LE BER F., LIGOZAT G., PAPINI O., *Raisonnements sur l'espace et le temps : des modèles aux applications*, Hermes-Lavoisier, Paris, 2007.

[ROB 65] ROBINSON J.A., "A machine-oriented logic based on the resolution principle", *Journal of the ACM (JACM)*, vol. 12, no. 1, pp. 23–41, 1965.

[SOU 06] SOULIGNAC V., BARNABÉ F., RAT D. *et al.*, "SIGEMO : un système d'information pour la gestion des épandages de matières organiques. Du cahier des charges à l'outil opérationnel", *Ingénieries-EAT*, vol. 47, pp. 37–42, 2006.

Reviewing the Qualifiers of Imperfection in Geographic Information

9.1. Introduction

Geographic analysis often has to deal with the gradual acquisition of information, allowing us to review time and again the state of our knowledge (inferred from the data available and our previous knowledge). This need is all the more acute as official geographic information – produced according to certified protocols (established by IGN, BRGM, INSEE, etc.) on specific dates – must be complemented by other types of information, especially Volunteered Geographic Information (VGI), which is produced continuously and affected by significantly more marked imperfections (incomplete, imprecise, uncertain, or even conflicting information). This chapter will tackle the belief revision methods used for imperfect information, especially Bayesian revision (Bayes' theorem and Jeffrey's rule) and the alternatives in non-probabilistic formalisms (Dempster's rule of combination in evidence theory, possibilistic conditioning in possibility theory). Thus, this chapter is closely related to Chapter 5, which presented various theories about the imperfect representation of spatial objects. This section shows how those theories can be implemented from an operational point of view, to solve the issue of belief revision on available information. Their respective advantages and shortfalls will also be highlighted, so as to reach the conclusion that each methodological approach can be more or less suitable in various contexts in relation to the knowledge of spatial information.

Chapter written by Giovanni FUSCO and Andrea TETTAMANZI.

A brief example will be presented in this section to illustrate the points in question. A city in a developing country has just been hit by a violent earthquake[1]. The official geographic information available is often obsolete or even non-existent in various areas. Information that is more or less complete and reliable emerges from the field through social networks. The authorities charged with managing the crisis intend to adapt this information for a geographic information system, to manage first aid as well as possible and constantly update the state of their knowledge about the damaged city.

We will see how the use of new geographic information can be adapted in various ways to manage this crisis. We will refer to some basic notions in knowledge engineering (KE) that have been incorporated over time into the field of spatial information management. A geographic information system may be conceived as a specific formalization of a knowledge base (we will identify later on the limitations of its formalism). Some types of knowledge may be understood as elements of what knowledge engineering calls *knowledge*: this is well-established knowledge that will not be questioned during the life cycle of a GIS and that is related in particular to the ontology of geographic objects (which geometric representations should be used for certain spatial objects, which structure should be employed for attribute tables, which identifiers, etc.). Other knowledge elements, especially the values provided in attribute tables and the coordinates that define spatial objects, may have more to do with what knowledge engineering calls *beliefs*: this is temporary knowledge and hypotheses that may be reviewed by the managers of the information system. In the following sections, we will first note that all the elements of this set of beliefs have binary truth values (true/false) and leave no room for uncertainty. We will see how, even in this scenario, revision operations may create imperfections in the set of beliefs. Afterward, we will consider the more general case in which clauses use from the very beginning formalisms employed for uncertain knowledge, and we will see how revision operations may take advantage of these formalisms to reach revised and consistent states of uncertain beliefs.

9.2. Belief revision and update in knowledge engineering

In knowledge engineering, we first distinguish between belief update and belief revision. The former refers to the expression of new beliefs to describe

---

1 The earthquake that hit Port-au-Prince (Haiti) in January 2010 with a Richter magnitude of 7.3 could be fairly similar to our imaginary example.

a new state of the physical world. New information does not replace older information, strictly speaking, as it refers to a description of a new spatiotemporal field. On the other hand, the latter involves taking into consideration new information elements (normally regarded as more reliable) so as to modify our beliefs about a single state of the world.

Let us suppose, for example, that the city hit by the earthquake has two dispensaries. We know their coordinates so that we can represent them at least as points in our GIS. An attribute column will provide information about the functional state of each dispensary. For example, one of two modalities (*functional* and *non-functional*) could be assigned to a variable. In the first version of the GIS, which models the state of the city before the earthquake, both dispensaries are functional. Knowing that, after the earthquake, dispensary 1 that has been destroyed implies updating the beliefs to produce a new version of the GIS. On the other hand, we can assume that the GIS that describes the city after the earthquake has by default considered that the two dispensaries were functional because their reinforced concrete structure is supposed to withstand the recorded magnitude of the earthquake. Some field evidence reveals that dispensary 1 has been destroyed and is therefore no longer functional. At this point, we have to proceed with a belief revision in the GIS that models the city after the earthquake, as a more recent (and, in this case, more reliable) information element has modified our belief in the description of the spatial object on the same date.

9.3. The limitations faced by GIS when representing a set of beliefs

We will now see which limitations GIS face when modeling a set of beliefs about a state of the world. Like all databases, a GIS includes a structure based on classes and instances that pair, unlike non-geographic databases, a double description – geometric and semantic – of spatial objects (see Chapter 6).

This type of database, once instantiated, could be seen as a set of propositions about the spatial objects (each instance of the GIS is one of them; for example, dispensary with coordinates $x1$ and $y1$ is functional), enabling a reasoning process based on propositional logic, and as a set of property of the objects (e.g. each dispensary has a date on which it became functional), defined by the structure of the geometry and the semantic attributes of each class of objects, enabling a reasoning process based on first-order logic.

In reality, this structure in n-tuples, which is typical of any classical database, is suitable only for the representation of information that corresponds to conjunctive clauses (e.g. dispensary 1 with coordinates $x1$ and $y2$ is functional AND dispensary 2 with coordinates $x2$ and $y2$ is functional). Thus, in a GIS, we cannot correctly represent information of a disjunctive type. Let us suppose, for example, that a tweet sent from the city devastated by the earthquake tells us that "the dispensary has been destroyed," without specifying whether it is dispensary 1 or 2 (the citizen who sent the message may not be aware that there are two dispensaries). As for the functional state of the dispensaries, which can be modeled by a binary variable, this information corresponds to the clause $(\neg n°1 \ V \ \neg n°2)$. We could consider filling in the field *functional state* of both dispensaries with the modality *functional V non-functional*. This representation does not correspond to the disjunctive clause $(\neg n°1 \ V \ \neg n°2)$, as it does not rule out that both dispensaries are still functional.

From this point of view, a GIS is not appropriate for the representation of any set of beliefs, but only of specific sets of beliefs that include only conjunctive clauses. To represent more generally a set of beliefs, it is necessary to pair the GIS with a set of other clauses (e.g. disjunctive) by using a less constraining representation language, for example, description logics (DL). In addition, these more expressive formal languages enable the use of an automatic reasoner for the logical closure of a set of beliefs (i.e. the inference of all the possible deductions based on the clauses included in a set) and ensure the consistency of the set (i.e. the lack of contradiction among clauses). Wesel and Möller [WES 03, WES 09] have suggested hybrid systems for combining the GIS with DL clauses that cannot be modeled by the GIS and a reasoner.

9.4. Revision in a set of binary beliefs

Let us consider now how a set of binary beliefs K (thus, some propositions that can only be thought to be true or false) can be modeled by a GIS, with the aforementioned limitations, or by a hybrid system that includes a GIS. When K refers to the same state of the world, the following operations may generally be carried out on it [GÄR 92]:

Expansion: the addition of one or more clauses to the existing clauses without verifying the consistency of the new set (including the logical deductions of the clauses reported). A GIS could, for example, be structured into two polygonal layers of information: the first contains the footprint of buildings, whereas the second includes the types of urban land cover (e.g. continuous urban fabric, discontinuous urban fabric, natural space or farmland pockmarked by urban sprawl, etc.). Adding new buildings to the first layer is an expansion of K, which could also include logical inconsistencies (adding a built-up area could require other operations on the layer of land-cover types, for example, if the new buildings create a new urban sprawl area).

– Contraction: the elimination of one or more clauses from the set (e.g. the elimination of instances) without verifying the consistency of the new set.

– Consolidation: an operation that involves restoring the consistency of a set of beliefs (solving logical inconsistencies).

– Revision: the addition of new beliefs while also ensuring logical consistency.

– Fusion: an operation that involves bringing together and consolidating different sets of beliefs so as to obtain a new logically consistent set.

Revision may be regarded as a specific case of fusion where new beliefs are prioritized over older beliefs, as they are considered more reliable. In a set of binary beliefs, a revision may then involve simply replacing old beliefs with new beliefs, while also eliminating the deductions made from the old beliefs and adding the deductions that derive from the new beliefs.

In knowledge engineering, the consistency of the revision operation is ensured by respecting the six basic postulates of the AGM reference framework, named after the three authors who formalized it [ALC 85]. When a new belief P is used to revise a set of beliefs K (the set after the revision is usually noted $K * P$), the AGM framework ensures more specifically the logical closure of the revision (all the logical consequences of the revised set must be included in the set of beliefs), its success (P must belong to the newly revised set), its inclusion (the revised set is included in the set produced by an expansion), its vacuity (if $\neg P$ did not belong to K, then expansion and revision would be equivalent), the non-addition of inconsistencies (the revised set will be inconsistent only if K or P was already inconsistent), and extensionality (if two new beliefs P and Q are logically equivalent, K may be revised by either). Only the revisions that respect the six postulates of the AGM framework are regarded as rational. Two further postulates, which concern revisions by compound beliefs, are accepted and implemented in the literature in various ways.

Let us suppose that we are revising our set of beliefs K about the state of the city after the earthquake according to the AGM framework. As has been pointed out, K was first instantiated with the two functional dispensaries. The disjunctive clause P $(\neg n°1$ V $\neg n°2)$ with which we aim to revise the beliefs in K may be regarded as the first case of imperfect information (it may be simultaneously interpreted as incomplete information or as imprecise information). The revision of K by P leads to a multiplicity of possible worlds, which are all compatible with the new set of beliefs $K * P$.

9.5. The case of uncertain beliefs

Chapter 5 illustrated the various formalisms used to represent imperfect information about geographic objects. More specifically, as for the uncertainty of geographic information, qualifying imperfection implies assigning plausibility values (this notion is meant here in its broadest sense) to the various possible worlds. In this respect, binary logic is left behind, as a clause may no longer be only true or false, but also characterized by an intermediate degree of plausibility.

Let us reconsider our example and suppose that we have to find out whether a bridge is functional after the devastating earthquake. In a set of binary beliefs, the attribute table can only be filled out with the values {yes, no} and possibly yes V no, which corresponds to a state of total ignorance and, therefore, to an empty box (left blank).

ID	Type	Usable
1	Bridge	

Table 9.1.

In a probabilistic representation of information, the attribute table includes a field *p(usable)* that quantifies the plausibility of the possible world in which the bridge is usable. The dual field *p(unusable)* is superfluous since, in the case of a binary variable, the Kolmogorov axioms guarantee that we can obtain the probability of the second modality as a complement to '1', the probability of the first modality. Thus, let us suppose that the manager of the GIS after the earthquake wants to consider the possibility that bridge is usable, as the literature reveals that bridges with the same structural characteristics, when hit by an earthquake of such magnitude, normally have a probability of 0.6 of withstanding the earthquake and remaining functional. Thus, the attribute table will look similar to the following:

ID	Type	p (usable)	p (unusable)
1	Bridge	0.6	0.4

Table 9.2.

Models that use Dempster–Shafer's evidence theory (see section 5.3.2) can include, more specifically, aspects related to intrinsic uncertainty, associated with the variability of the event (bridges with the same characteristics when hit by this type of earthquake may remain usable or not with an odds ratio of 3:2), and those linked to the epistemic uncertainty of the modeler (it is not certain that the statistical model available can appropriately describe this bridge since, e.g. it is not known how old it is, or the micro-seismic situation may be much more significant than the structural strength of the bridge).

Thus, the modeler will assign a belief mass to the various subsets of the possible worlds, for example, 0.5 to the fact that the statistical model does not apply to the case in question, and 0.3 and 0.2 to the two modalities *usable* and *unusable*, according to the odds ratio of the statistical model. Following the theory explained in Chapter 5, these belief masses (whose sum is always a unit sum, as is the case for probabilities) are used to calculate a belief and a plausibility for the various events (as illustrated in Table 9.3). The terms "belief" and "plausibility" are used here in the very specific sense employed in Dempster–Shafer's theory [SHA 76] and correspond to the lower and upper boundaries, corroborated by the evidence available, of poorly known probabilities of each event.

Event	Mass	Belief	Plausibility
Usable bridge	0.3	0.3	0.8
Unusable bridge	0.2	0.2	0.7
Usable or unusable bridge	0.5	1	1

Table 9.3.

The attribute table for the bridge in question will look similar to the following:

ID	Type	bel (usable)	pl (usable)	bel (unusable)	pl (unusable)
1	Bridge	0.3	0.8	0.2	0.7

Table 9.4.

Like in the probabilistic case, the fields related to the second modality of a binary variable are superfluous, since bel (unusable) and pl (unusable) can be calculated, based on the belief and plausibility of the first modality according to the relations:

$$\text{Bel}\,(\neg A) = 1 - \text{Pl}(A) \qquad\qquad [9.1a]$$

$$\text{Pl}\,(\neg A) = 1 - \text{Bel}(A). \qquad\qquad [9.1b]$$

As was the case in evidence theory, possibility theory makes it peasible to model the beliefs of the knowing agent with a pair of measures, in this case necessity and possibility, which constitute the lower and upper boundaries of poorly known probabilities (see section 5.3.3). In fact, the two theories may be regarded as specific cases of the imprecise probability theory [WAL 91], which models the poor knowledge of a probability distribution in the most general terms. As was the case for probability theory, in possibility theory, expert knowledge is elicited only for elementary events and not for the power set of the possible worlds. Possibility theory, especially in its qualitative version, is particularly suitable for representation of uncertain knowledge assessed only in terms of the degree of plausibility. The possibility scale Π measures here the degree to which an expert is not surprised about an elementary event: $\Pi = 1$ corresponds to a completely normal event, which is therefore utterly unsurprising; $\Pi = 0$ corresponds to an impossible event; $\Pi = 0.8$ may characterize a relatively ordinary event, which is therefore fairly unsurprising; and $\Pi = 0.2$ corresponds to a nearly impossible event, which is therefore very surprising. What matters in this qualitative assessment is not the precise value of the possibility measure, but the order established by these values between the various modalities of a variable. On the other hand, the necessity measure N is a degree of certainty about information: $N = 1$ corresponds to absolute certainty and $N = 0$ to a total lack of certainty. Information with $N > 0$ is regarded as true, but not completely certain (unless $N = 1$).

The attribute table shown below regards the usable state of the bridge after the earthquake as entirely normal, given its structural characteristics and the magnitude of the earthquake. The fact that the bridge is unusable is not considered normal, but not very surprising either ($\Pi = 0.6$). These assessments could correspond to a qualitative elicitation that is not necessarily corroborated by statistical information.

ID	Type	Π (usable)	N (usable)	Π (unusable)	N (unusable)
1	bridge	1	0.4	0.6	0

Table 9.5.

As was the case for modeling in evidence theory, the fields related to the second modality of a binary variable are superfluous, since Π (unusable) and N (unusable) can be calculated based on the possibility and the necessity of the first modality according to the relations:

$$\Pi(\neg A) = 1 - N(A) \tag{9.2a}$$

$$N(\neg A) = 1 - \Pi(A). \tag{9.2b}$$

When information is uncertain, revising the qualifiers of imperfection involves revising the values of probabilities, beliefs/plausibilities, or possibilities/necessities by considering the new information provided to the manager of geographic information, while also respecting the AGM formal framework. In terms of calculations, this revision looks like a conditioning process, as the issue is to calculate new probability/plausibility/possibility values, depending on the knowledge of the new information elements. The conditioning process may, in fact, be understood as a specific case of belief revision, traditionally limited to the revision of uncertain qualifiers when new and certain information is available but later extended to include the case in which new information is in turn uncertain.

9.6. Bayesian probabilistic conditioning

Probabilistic conditioning relies on Bayes' theorem and enables the revision of a subjective probability depending on the observation of a piece of empirical evidence (in this case, the new information). Bayes' theorem is based on the relation between the joint probability of two events (A and B) and the conditional probability of an event in relation to the other:

$$p(A \cap B) = p(B|A)\, p(A) = p(A|B)\, p(B). \tag{9.3}$$

In a conditioning operation, we normally assign an asymmetric role to the various knowledge elements: there is a prior probability distribution $p(H_i)$ over some hypotheses H_i (the modalities of a variable H which are therefore uncertain), and we obtain a certain piece of information E (evidence) for which $p(E) = 1$, entailing a revision of our beliefs $p(H_i)$. Bayes' theorem can then be formalized as follows:

$$p(H_i|\, E) = \frac{p(E|H_i)p(H_i)}{\sum_i \ p(E|H_i)p(H_i)}. \tag{9.4}$$

$p(H_i|E)$ is the posterior probability distribution of the hypotheses, namely, the one that follows the revision, when E is known. Some crucial elements involved in calculating Bayesian conditioning are the likelihoods $p(E|H_i)$ that quantify the probabilities based on which the various hypotheses have generated the evidence E (they do not add up to 1 as each time the probabilistic model changes). As Shafer noted [SHA 81], the knowledge of these likelihoods is not always guaranteed in concrete cases, and it limits the use of Bayesian probabilistic models much more than prior probabilistic approximations, which are in any case designed for constant revision as new information becomes available.

Bayes' theorem, as a probabilistic conditioning rule, may be generalized to the case in which the evidence E is not certain but there is a probability distribution q on a relatively basic partition of the sample space of E. The posterior probability to estimate is now $q(H_i|E)$ and Jeffrey's rule generalizes Bayes' theorem as follows:

$$q(H_i \mid E) = \sum_j \ q_j p\big(H_i \mid E_j\big) \tag{9.5}$$

where each $p(H_i|E_j)$ is calculated according to equation [9.3].

Following Jeffrey's rule, the asymmetry between prior probability distribution and certain evidence is eliminated, since the evidence is also affected by uncertainty.

Let us reconsider our example. During the assessment of the functional condition of the bridge, for which we have already expressed our prior probabilities (Table 8), a citizen's account from the field, deemed to be reliable, indicates that the bridge is unusable. Let us see how Bayesian conditioning may be used for the revision of the prior probabilities. We can employ Bayes' theorem [9.4]. The essential elements for the calculations are the two likelihoods $p(E|unusable)$ and $p(E|usable)$. The evidence is the account of a non-expert observer who reported that the bridge is unusable. Thus, we need a statistical model that allows us to quantify how probable it is that a bridge, which is unusable after an earthquake, is perceived as being unusable by a non-expert (like our informant). A second model should tell us how probable it is that a bridge which is usable after an earthquake, following some superficial changes that do not compromise its functional state (surface cracks, minor damage, etc.), is perceived as being unusable by a non-expert. Let us suppose that those values correspond to 0.9 and 0.2, respectively (as we have pointed out, the sum of the likelihoods is not a unit sum, as these probabilities derive from different models). Thus, we can calculate:

$$p(\text{unusable}|\ E) = \frac{0,9\ x\ 0,4}{0,9\ x\ 0,4+0,2\ x\ 0,6} = 0.75.$$

Thus, the new attribute table will look like this:

ID	Type	p (usable)	p (unusable)
1	Bridge	0.25	0.75

Table 9.6.

Our probabilistic belief in the fact that the bridge is unusable, after taking into consideration the observer's account, has changed from 0.4 to 0.75. Thanks to probabilistic conditioning, the evidence E has made it possible to revise our belief. This does not simply involve replacing an old belief with a new one.

One of the advantages of Bayesian conditioning is its recursiveness. For example, let us suppose that a new account E_2, which has become available to us, states that the bridge is usable. The current prior probability distribution now corresponds to 0.25 for a usable bridge and 0.75 for an unusable bridge. The likelihoods that we have already used also allow us to calculate $p(E_2|usable) = 0.8$ and $p(E_2|unusable) = 0.1$. Thus, we can calculate:

$$p(\text{usable}|\ E) = \frac{0.80 \times 0.25}{0.8 \times 0.25 + 0.1 \times 0.75} = 0.727.$$

After the new revision, the attribute table will become:

ID	Type	p (usable)	p (unusable)
1	Bridge	0.727	0.273

Table 9.7.

The order of the two revisions has no effect on the final result. The asymmetry in the likelihoods (it is slightly more likely to make a mistake by regarding as unusable a bridge which is actually still functional than by incorrectly regarding as usable a bridge that is severely damaged) results in the fact that the revision of the prior probabilities made by the two conflicting accounts slightly reinforces the belief in the fact that the bridge is usable (it increases from 0.6 to 0.727). The precision of the probabilistic calculation is simultaneously the strong point and the limitation of this formalism. To the extent that prior probabilities and likelihoods do not result from statistical calculations but from the elicitations of experts, these values, which are often approximate, can then be used in deceptively precise quantitative calculations.

Bayesian conditioning, on the other hand, benefits from the availability of a highly sophisticated mathematization. If the likelihood functions can be modeled by a binomial (a binary variable) or multinomial (a variable with n-values) distribution, then the conjugate prior distribution theory [RAI 61] allows us to use the Beta or the Dirichlet distribution. In these functions, the equivalent experience of the prior distributions (which quantifies the experience accumulated by the expert to formulate these probabilities) and the number of observations that corroborate each piece of evidence entered in the model can be easily integrated into the calculations as hyperparameters [BOL 07]. Thus, we can carry out highly sophisticated belief revisions of this kind: given a prior distribution, equivalent to the experience of 50 observations, for a probability of 0.4 that the bridge is unusable after such an earthquake, how can this probability be revised given that according to 10 accounts the bridge is unusable while according to 2 it is usable?

9.7. Revision in evidence theory

As Shafer underlines [SHA 81], both Bayesian probability theory and evidence theory should be conceived as two models built to meet representational needs in the contexts of specific bodies of knowledge. Bayesian probability theory does so by comparing the events to be modeled to canonical examples with known probabilities and likelihood functions. Evidence theory does so by comparing the events to be modeled with canonical examples which are messages with a known probability of corroborating a specific event. We could thus consider the example of new information about the city devastated by the earthquake in the form of a message that can be analyzed as an aerial image of the bridge. Unfortunately, the image is of poor quality, and the experts think that they have found in it some elements that can support the hypothesis that the bridge is unusable, but it is also equally possible that these elements are artifacts deriving from the poor image. Thus, we can distribute the probability mass equal to a message that supports the hypothesis that the bridge is unusable and to another message that is still compatible with the two independent events. According to evidence theory, the aerial image presents the following informational content:

Event	Mass	Belief	Plausibility
Usable bridge	0	0	0.5
Unusable bridge	0.5	0.5	1
Usable or unusable bridge	0.5	1	1

Table 9.8.

Conditioning the beliefs and plausibilities presented in Table 9.3 with this new information involves merging first the subjacent belief masses with those deriving from the aerial image. This can be done with Dempster's rule of combination [SHA 76]. Thus, conditioning in evidence theory is conceived from the beginning of the case in which evidence is uncertain. For an event A, given two mass belief distributions $m_1(A)$ and $m_2(A)$, the fusion of the belief masses $m_{1,2}(A)$ is given by:

$$m_{1,2}(A) = \frac{1}{1-K} \sum_{B \cap C = A \neq 0} m_1(B)\, m_2(C) \qquad [9.6]$$

where

$$K = \sum_{B \cap C = 0} m_1(B)\, m_2(C). \qquad [9.7]$$

In our example, $K = 0.3 \times 0.5 = 0.15$. It represents the product of the belief mass equal to 0.3 in the first distribution, corresponding to the fact that the bridge is unusable. It also represents in the second distribution, the product of the belief mass equal to 0.5, corresponding to the fact that the bridge is unusable. Therefore, the standardization factor is equal to 1.176.

K is a measure of the level of conflict between the two mass distributions. Dempster's rule of combination implies calculating all the combinations of pieces of evidence that corroborate a given event in the two mass distributions and standardizing then the resulting masses based on the common beliefs for the two distributions, namely, ignoring the conflicts between them.

Thus, for the new mass to assign to the event that the bridge is not usable, we obtain:

$$m_{1,2}(\text{unusable}) = 1.176 \times (0.2 \times 0.5 + 0.5 \times 0.5 + 0.2 \times 0.5) = 0.529.$$

After all these calculations, we obtain the new table resulting from the fusion:

Event	Mass	Belief	Plausibility
Usable bridge	0.177	0.176	0.471
Unusable bridge	0.529	0.529	0.823
Usable or unusable bridge	0.294	1	1

Table 9.9.

Thus, we can see that the ignorance, expressed by the mass assigned to the fact that the bridge may be either usable or unusable, has considerably decreased: the two mass distributions assigned a value of 0.5 to this event, but the new distribution after their fusion assigns a mass of only 0.294 to it. Correspondingly, the differences between the plausibilities and the beliefs of the two elementary events have reduced, decreasing from 0.5 to around 0.3. Naturally, it is the elementary event "unusable bridge" that increases its plausibility and belief in relation to Table 9.3.

Fundamentally, the goal of information aggregation is to provide a meaningful and consistent summary of a body of data, whether it derives from one or more sources. A rule of combination is a special type of aggregation operator that processes data produced by multiple sources. Dempster's rule of combination is based on the hypothesis that these sources are independent and that their assessment is reliable. This would be the case if, for example, the sources were a panel of independent experts who may express different but complementary points of view, which rely on the same objective reality. In this case, underlining the areas of agreement between the sources and ignoring any conflicting evidence is justified. It is like establishing a logical conjunction of the sources' opinions. All the experts are right, even if their statements are not the same: at most, when considered one by one, they are not precise enough. On the contrary, when a source is thought to be reliable and the others are not, the logical operation that can be justifiably carried out is logical disjunction (one of the sources is right, but no one knows which). There is a continuum of compensatory combination operators between conjunction and disjunction. We can see that Dempster's rule is situated at one end of this continuum.

Not taking into consideration the level of conflict between two mass distributions, when this level is significant, is an approach that has been seriously criticized [YAG 87], [ZAD 86]. In fact, a large number of alternative rules of combination, some of which are parametric, have been suggested in the literature (for a survey of some of them, see [SEN 02]).

9.8. Possibilistic conditioning

As is the case for the probability theory, possibilistic conditioning that involves certain evidence derives from the relation between joint and conditional possibilities of two events:

$$\Pi(A \cap B) = \Pi(B|A) * \Pi(A) \tag{9.8}$$

where * corresponds to *min* in subjective qualitative possibilities and to the product in quantitative possibilities derived from statistical calculations. If the operator *min* is considered, equation [9.8] does not have a unique solution. Thus, the least specific solution, i.e. the solution with the largest degree of possibility that respects the constraint of equation [9.8], is chosen. The possibility distribution underlying the conditional possibility measure Π (B|A) is [DUB 97]:

$$\pi(\omega|A) = \begin{cases} 1 & if \ \pi(\omega) = \Pi(A) > 0, \ \omega \in A \\ 0 & if \ \omega \notin A \\ \pi(\omega) & if \ \pi(\omega) < \Pi(A), \quad \omega \in A \end{cases} \qquad [9.9]$$

Thus, the possibility of a possible world ω conditional on the knowledge of the event A is:

– Total (hence completely unsurprising), if ω is included in A, and if its prior possibility is as significant as the prior possibility of A.

– Equal to zero, if ω is incompatible with A.

– Unchanged, if ω is included in A but with a prior possibility smaller than that of A.

This entails that Π (B|A) = Π(A∩B) if Π(A∩B) < Π (A), and that Π (B|A) = 1 if Π(A∩B) = Π (A) > 0.

For quantitative possibilities, where the operator * corresponds to the product, it is possible to calculate:

$$\Pi(B|A) = \frac{\Pi(A \cap B)}{\Pi(A)} \qquad [9.10]$$

This relation is valid regardless of *B*, provided that Π(A) > 0, since the value of *A* may be possibly highly surprising, even though it will not be impossible (the evidence has just been produced). Dubois and Prade [DUB 97] note that equation [9.10] corresponds to the conditioning of Dempster's rule of combination specified for possibility measures.

The posterior possibility distribution that corresponds to equation [9.10] is:

$$\pi(\omega|A) = \begin{cases} \dfrac{\pi(\omega)}{\Pi(A)} & if \quad \omega \in A \\ 0 & if \quad \omega \notin A \end{cases}.$$ [9.11]

The same authors [DUB 97] also show that the possibilistic conditioning of equations [9.9] and [9.10] respect the AGM postulates and can be thus formally understood as revisions of rational beliefs in the sense meant by the AGM.

Even possibilistic conditioning may be generalized to the case that concerns uncertain evidence so as to obtain the equivalent of the probabilistic conditioning of Jeffrey's rule [DUB 97]. If A is a binary variable, we obtain uncertain evidence for event A, with a necessity measure equal to $N(A) = \alpha$, which means that in the posterior possibility measure Π', $\Pi'(A) = 1$ and $\Pi'(\neg A)=1 - \alpha$. $N(A)$ is the degree of certainty of the event A. In this case:

$$\pi(\omega \,|\, (A, \alpha))= \max \, (\pi(\omega \,|\, A), (1 - \alpha)* \pi(\omega \,|\, \neg A))$$ [9.12]

where $*$ is the min in qualitative possibilities and the product in quantitative possibilities, and $\pi(\omega \,|\, A)$ is calculated according to equation [9.9] or [9.11].

In the more general case of a variable with multiple modalities, the uncertainty about the evidence can be expressed as a series of possibility measures $\Pi(A_i)=\lambda_i$ with $\max(\lambda_i) = 1$. The possibilistic equivalent of Jeffrey's rule is then:

$$\pi(\omega \,|\, \{(A_i, \lambda_i)\})= \max \, (\lambda_i * \pi(\omega \,|\, A_i)).$$ [9.13]

Thus, it can be noted that the generalization of the conditioning process for the variables with multiple modalities preferably employs the possibility measures λ_i. This is instead of the necessity measure α used in the binary case, because λ_i plays the same role in equation [9.13] as $1 - \alpha$ does in equation [9.12].

Therefore, we will use equation [9.12] for the revision of the possibilistic beliefs about the functional state of the bridge presented in Table 9.5. Qualitative possibility theory allows us to qualitatively assess the plausibility of its usability when statistical information is lacking (the likelihoods) by asking the sources how sure they are of their information. Let us imagine, for example, that the informant who has observed the bridge after the earthquake tells us simultaneously that, according to him, the bridge is unusable and that he is relatively confident in his statement. This could correspond to a necessity measure $\alpha = 0.6$. Thus, we can calculate:

Π (usable | (unusable, 0.6)) =
max (π(usable | unusable), min(0.4 , π(usable | usable)) = 0.4

Π (unusable | (unusable, 0.6)) =
max (π(unusable | unusable), min(0.4 , π(unusable | usable)) = 1.

The belief revision that follows the conditioning leads us now to consider the fact that the bridge is unusable as completely plausible and to assign a certain degree of surprise to the fact that it is usable, inverting the prior beliefs seen in Table 9.5. It can be noted that if we had obtained n times the same evidence with the same certainty α, the result would have always been the same.

Let us imagine now, as was the case in the probabilistic example, that a second source reports that the bridge is usable with a degree of certainty $\alpha = 0.8$. Considering that the prior distribution is now Π (usable) = 0.4 and Π (unusable) = 1, repeatedly applying equation [9.12] yields:

Π (usable | (usable, 0.8)) =
max (π(usable | usable), min(0.2 , π(usable | unusable)) = 1

Π (unusable | (usable, 0,8)) =
max (π(unusable | usable), min(0.2 , π(unusable | unusable)) = 0.2.

Thus, the iterated application of [9.12] in a qualitative context seems to involve the replacement of a belief with another, rather than sophisticated conditioning of the values. The problem with our example is that the variable is binary and that each observation, even when not completely certain, makes the unobserved modality surprising.

We need to consider a slightly more complex example, and potentially to introduce quantitative possibilities, in order to fully appreciate the ability of possibilistic conditioning to combine prior beliefs with uncertain evidence. We wish to fill in, in our GIS after the earthquake, the functional state of the bridge with a slightly more detailed model: a functional bridge could be perfectly functional (this would imply that it could be used to its maximum bearing capacity) or less functional than it is supposed to be (this would force us to limit its capacity when the bridge is open to traffic); a bridge that is no longer functional could, in turn, run the risk of collapsing (this would force us to cordon off the area for security reasons) or it could be unusable without any threat of collapse (in that case, it would only be closed to traffic). An observer in the field cannot distinguish between these aspects and will keep reporting that the bridge is usable or that it is not usable.

Let us consider at first the context of qualitative possibilities. After the experts' assessment of the ability of the bridge to withstand the earthquake that has taken place, the prior possibility distribution is the following:

		Usable bridge		Unusable bridge	
ID	Type	Π (perfect state)	Π (reduced functional state)	Π (no threat of collapse)	Π (threat of collapse)
1	bridge	0.8	1	0.6	0.4

Table 9.10.

Thus, according to the experts, it is perfectly normal that the bridge can be used with the reduced functional state, and they would be very surprised if the bridge ran the risk of collapsing.

The report from the field, according to which the bridge is unusable, with certainty $\alpha = 0.8$, implies using the conditioning presented in equation [9.13] to calculate $\pi(\omega \mid \{(\text{usable}, 0.2), (\text{unusable}, 1)\})$, where ω is, in turn, one of the four possible worlds reported in the GIS.

For the case of the bridge being in perfect state, we obtain:

Π (perfect state $\mid \{(\text{usable}, 0.2), (\text{unusable}, 1)\}) =$
max (min(0.2, π(perfect state $\mid$ usable)), min(1, π(perfect state $\mid$ unusable))) =
max (min(0.2, 0.8), min(1, 0)) =0.2.

The conditional possibilities for the other three modalities can be calculated in the same way, leading to a new attribute table that includes the posterior possibility values:

ID	Type	Usable bridge		Unusable bridge	
		Π (perfect state)	Π (reduced functional state)	Π (no threat of collapse)	Π (threat of collapse)
1	bridge	0.2	0.2	1	0.4

Table 9.11.

The normal and completely possible event now involves the bridge in an unusable state with no threat of collapse, as it corresponds to the least surprising state in keeping with the empirical evidence. The two states that correspond to the usable bridge (perfect state and reduced functional state) become very surprising: their possibility corresponds to the residual uncertainty about the empirical evidence. In terms of possibility, the state that involves the threat of collapse is the second event. Assessing the plausibilities of the states of the bridge must involve a strictly ordinal type of logic, as the qualitative possibility theory does not assign a specific meaning to the numerical values of the possibilities.

On the other hand, in the context of quantitative possibilities, the experts could support the possibilities shown in Table 9.10, thanks to statistical elements. If we (quite unrealistically) hypothesized that the observer in the field can also provide a certainty value $\alpha = 0.8$ supported by statistical factors (such as likelihoods in probabilistic revision), equation [9.11] could then be used in equation [9.13].

For example, considering the case in which the bridge runs the risk of collapsing:

$$\Pi \text{ (threat of collapse} \mid \{(\text{usable, } 0.2), (\text{unusable, } 1)\}) =$$
$$\max (0.2 \times \pi(\text{threat of collapse} \mid \text{usable})), 1 \times \pi(\text{threat of collapse} \mid$$
$$\text{unusable}))) = \max ((0.2 \times 0), (1 \times (0.4/0.6))) = 0.67.$$

Proceeding in the same manner for the other possible worlds, the new attribute table that contains the posterior possibility values will be the following:

ID	Type	Usable bridge		Unusable bridge	
		Π (perfect state)	Π (reduced functional state)	Π (no threat of collapse)	Π (threat of collapse)
1	bridge	0.16	0.2	1	0.67

Table 9.12.

Quantitative possibilistic conditioning makes it possible to interpret the differences and relations of possibility measures. Thus, we can appreciate the slight difference between the levels of surprise of the two possible worlds that are in conflict with the report from the field and, even more, the fact that the possibilities that the – unusable – bridge runs the risk of collapsing or not have the same 2:3 ratio that they had *a priori*.

9.9. Conclusion

We have seen that the qualifiers of imperfection in geographic information can be reviewed in the highly formalized framework of AGM belief revision in knowledge engineering. More specifically, pairing a GIS that can model only conjunctive clauses with a more expressive base could model significantly richer sets of beliefs about the state of the geographic space.

We have also presented the application of three different formalisms, with their revision procedures, used to model beliefs about geographic objects when their imperfections imply uncertainty. These formalisms are probability theory with Bayesian conditioning, evidence theory with Dempster's rule of combination, and possibility theory – qualitative and quantitative – with possibilistic conditioning. These revision procedures can easily integrate information elements that are in turn uncertain so as to obtain new knowledge states, which can be more or less uncertain, about geographic objects and their position in space.

It seems evident that each formalism may be preferable depending on the context of knowledge in question. In particular, if we can rely on statistical information to calibrate our uncertainties and if we can confidently adapt these statistical models to the phenomena studied, then modeling the qualifiers of imperfection and their revision will clearly benefit from using

Bayesian probabilities and Bayesian conditioning. Bayesian probabilities have the undeniable advantage of presenting significant mathematical sophistication in the models developed, for example, making it easy to integrate into conditioning the equivalent experience together with the prior beliefs and multiple evidence from the field. Yet, the availability of statistical information required (especially likelihoods even more than prior probabilities) could represent a critical element for the use of a probabilistic framework.

The combination of statistical information (especially in messages that inform us of the state of the geographic space) and uncertainty about the suitability of these statistical models for the phenomena studied finds a suitable formalism in Dempster–Shafer's evidence theory. This formalism also offers a good solution when uncertain data are merged, i.e. whenever we have the same level of confidence in the various sources. However, the attribution of belief masses and their combinations raise significant computing challenges. These operations must be carried out on the power set of the sample space whose cardinality may become extremely important when we consider the combinations of various events that are not necessarily binary. These practical considerations have tended to slow down the applied developments of evidence theory in geomatics.

Ultimately, possibility theory and possibilistic conditioning offer an alternative that is particularly suitable for cases in which geographic information derives only from the elicitations of experts. Once again, we can identify two scenarios. If experts can support possibility (non-surprise) and necessity (certainty) values with statistical information, quantitative possibility theory can be used to obtain the lower and upper boundaries of poorly known probabilities. The numerical values of possibilities and necessities may be revised by calculations that closely resemble the Bayesian framework and that may be compared quantitatively. On the other hand, if experts can only organize the possible worlds in terms of a limited number of levels of possibility/necessity, the qualitative possibility theory will provide the most appropriate representation. Thus, qualitative possibilistic conditioning will make it possible to revise the qualifiers of uncertainty by using only comparisons between levels. Although less expressive, this still remains the only suitable model for a framework characterized by high epistemic uncertainty. This can often be the case when managing crises and using VGI almost in real time, as we have illustrated in the example considered throughout this chapter.

9.10. References

[ALC 85] ALCHOURRON C., GÄRDENFORS P., MAKINSON D., "On the logic of theory change: partial meet contraction and revision functions", *The Journal of Symbolic Logic*, no. 50, pp. 510–530, 1985.

[BOL 07] BOLSTAD W., *Introduction to Bayesian Statistics*, 2nd Ed., John Wiley & Sons, Inc., Hoboken, NJ, 2007.

[DUB 97] DUBOIS D., PRADE H., "A synthetic view of belief revision with uncertain inputs in the framework of possibility theory", *International Journal of Approximate Reasoning*, vol. 1997, no. 17, pp. 295–324, 1997.

[GÄR 92] GÄRDENFORS P., "Belief revision: a vade-mecum", in PETTOROSSI A. (ed), *Meta-Programming in Logic. META 1992. Lecture Notes in Computer Science*, vol. 649, Springer, Berlin, Heidelberg, 1992.

[RAI 61] RAIFFA H., SCHLAIFER R., *Applied Statistical Decision Theory*, Division of Research, Graduate School of Business Administration, Harvard University, Cambridge, MA, 1961.

[SEN 02] SENTZ K., FERSON S., Combination of Evidence in Dempster–Shafer Theory, Technical report SAND 2002-0835, Sandia National Laboratories, Albuquerque, NM and Livermore, CA, 2002.

[SHA 76] SHAFER G., *A Mathematical Theory of Evidence*, Princeton University Press, Princeton, NJ, 1976.

[SHA 81] SHAFER G., "Jeffrey's rule of conditioning", *Philosophy of Science*, no. 48, pp. 337–362, 1981.

[WAL 91] WALLEY P., *Statistical Reasoning with Imprecise Probabilities*, Chapman and Hall, London, 1991.

[WES 03] WESSEL M., "Some practical issues in building a hybrid deductive geographic information system with a DL-Component", in *Proceedings of the 10th International Workshop on Knowledge Representation meets Databases (KRDB 2003)*, CEUR Workshop Proceedings, no. 79, 2003.

[WES 09] WESSEL M., MÖLLER R., "Flexible software architectures for ontology-based information systems", *Journal of Applied Logic*, Special Issue on Empirically Successful Systems, vol. 7, no. 1, pp. 75–99, 2009.

[YAG 87] YAGER R., "On the Dempster–Shafer framework and new combination rules", *Information Sciences*, no. 41, pp. 93–137, 1987.

[ZAD 86] ZADEH L., "A simple view of the Dempster–Shafer theory of evidence and its implication for the rule of combination", *The AI Magazine*, no. 7, pp. 85–90, 1986.

The Features of Decision Aid and Analysis Processes in Geography: How to Grasp Complexity, Uncertainty, and Risks?

10.1. The decision-making context

Part and parcel of a geographer's profession is being consulted about, or caught and involved in, issues that concern third parties who need an expert assessment of a territory before taking decisions.

For anyone, deciding means making choices and taking risks that potentially entail gains or losses. Deciding in an uncertain context and in a complex situation implies higher risks for the person who makes the decision.

Making decisions about a territory is rarely a simple issue. A decision-maker acts on public, collective, or communal spaces with history, morphology, various uses, etc. In this respect, the decision-maker must take into consideration, besides the territory affected by his decision, the lived and perceived multiplicity of territories of the actors implied or affected by the consequences of the decision.

In that context, a geographer's expertise may involve decision analysis (decision aid). The term "decision analysis" (decision aid) is not limited to the production of a tool used in geographic analysis, a monograph, or a map. Decision analysis refers to a process whereby a geographer helps one or more decision-makers or group of actors, who have previously asked for an

Chapter written by Myriam MERAD.

expert opinion, (i) define the issues, uncertainties, risks, and consequences of the request; (ii) formally model the request in its complexity; and (iii) express robust conclusions.

Thus, in decision analysis and in addition to geographic knowledge, a geographer must simultaneously be an expert (possess knowledge, know-how, and social skills) in the modes and measures that involve dialoguing and mediating between decision-makers and the actors of the territory, the formal models used to characterize and consider the inherent information, bodies of knowledge, uncertainties, the models that support joint collective decisions, and the identification of the long-term consequences of these decisions. In this regard, a geographer is responsible for the conditions of validity and legitimacy of their expertise [MER 13b]. The condition of validity refers to respecting the normative properties of the concepts and formal methods and approaches employed by a geographer. The condition of legitimacy refers to the need to take into account the expectations and usages of the parties involved as well as the aspects related to the long-term operability of the expertise involved.

In the context of this chapter, we will tackle the way in which decision analysis takes into consideration uncertainties, representations, and perceptions. We will illustrate how modeling these aspects may vary according to the geo-governance modes [BLE 13] imposed on the territory [DUB 15] or the modes of governance established by a decision-maker or implemented by a geographer to interact with the actors of the territory.

We have chosen to provide an overview of a type of method used to implement decision analysis: multiple-criteria decision-making methods. We will show how multiple-criteria aggregation procedures (MCAPs) may be chosen depending on one category of decision-analysis issues, namely, risk assessments that bring together risk analysis and risk management.

10.2. Geographers, decision-makers, actors, and the territory

Once a decision-maker has been explicitly requested, they become a party of a contract that obliges the two sides to provide a certain number of integral elements: the decision-maker agrees to spell out their operational issue and provide the available information, while the contracting party (henceforth referred to as the analyst) commits themselves to shedding light on the matter and carrying out decision analysis, aiming to help the decision-maker by providing them with the necessary elements for an informed decision (Figure 10.1).

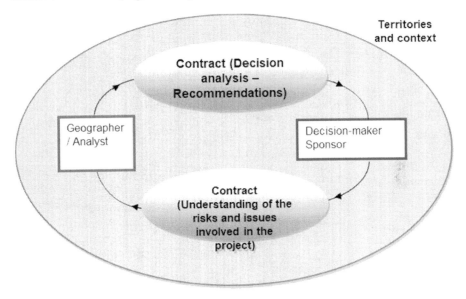

Figure 10.1. *The decision-support process – the nature of the relation between decision-maker and analyst (adapted from [MER 13])*

A geographer is not like any other analyst: besides knowing and expertly choosing the formal tools used to model a decision and in addition to their knowledge of the maieutic methods employed to draw out knowledge in complex situations, they have a different relationship with space. Thus, whereas a classic analyst regards the territory as input data whose area is ultimately determined by the decision-maker – in short, the territory is the space that may be affected by the decision-maker's actions – a geographer defines space in both its geographic and political, economic, social, cultural, and historical specific features. In this sense, the territory is simultaneously a decision object determined by the decision-maker and a party fully involved in the decision. This specific characteristic makes a geographer an analyst who pays attention to both the validity of the formal models that they will implement when using their expertise and the establishment of a legitimacy and legitimization element of what may contribute to the creation of a robust and viable decision.

Let us reconsider what is at the source of the contract: the decision-maker. This actor is commonly mistaken for the sponsor of the study. This confusion, which is far from trivial, may result in a reduction of the "decision-analysis" space to the issue (problem) as it is strictly formulated and established by the sponsor. Becoming aware of this difference allows a geographer to open the decision-analysis field and include support for the identification and structuring of issues.

Once the pair (Sponsor, Analyst) has been formed, the issue (problem) concerns the identification and the involvement of the parties involved in the territory affected by the decision in question.

At this stage, the analysts' practices vary. For some of them, the actors and parties implied, who have been identified and considered, are those identified by the sponsor as necessarily involved. According to others, the actors and parties involved are simultaneously those who are involved and affected, whether directly or indirectly, both visible and invisible in the territory affected by the decision. The notion of invisibility refers to the fact that, beyond the physical presence of the actors in the space affected by the decision, there are other actors who are either involved in or are affected by the decisions and who are situated outside this area. In a way, this sheds light on the fact that the territory affected by the decision is not a neutral object but a political object, in the sense of societal politics, whose definition has an effect mostly on the legitimacy of the decision and, consequently, on its validity.

10.3. The objects, stakes, and issues involved in a decision

We have previously seen that it is much more complex to define the territory affected by a decision analysis than the mere object of a contract. It is now necessary to establish the objects involved in the decision. The "decision objects", defined based on the contexts and cases as "actions", "scenarios", and "areas", are the elementary objects identified by a sponsor or an analyst as the objects that should be analyzed and on which the findings of the decision analysis will focus. These objects may be, for example, portfolios of stocks that will have to be examined in terms of risk assessment, banks whose ability to recover from potential financial shocks should be assessed, industrial plants whose security level should be identified, the viability or sustainability of energy scenarios, or wildfire-prone swathes of forests. Decision objects may be spatial or immaterial objects.

How a sponsor chooses to define and select these decision objects also affects the legitimization of the decision and decision analysis process. In fact, it is through and in relation to these objects, which may be qualified as "artifacts" of the interaction and negotiation between "the decision-maker, the sponsor, the analyst, the actors, and the parties involved", that the stakes of these parties can be directly or indirectly identified. The stakes are, in this case, significant elements for one or several actors who run risks (of gain or loss) in light of the actions that may be taken and implemented by the decision-maker.

These important elements may be explicit or implicit. It is the analyst's task to figure out or reveal these stakes as the decision issue is defined and structured.

Defining and structuring the decision issue (problem)	
1	Describing the request and the territory defined by the decision-maker
2	Describing the history of the territory
3	Identifying the decision level
4	Defining information and knowledge
5	Defining the uncertainties
6	Defining the stakes and constraints related and unrelated to expertise
7	Identifying and analyzing the interplay of actors and organizations
8	Carrying out a contextual analysis (risks and resistance) and examining how critical the context is

Figure 10.2. *The first phase in decision analysis: defining and structuring the decision issue*

The individual requesting the expertise may have a clear picture of the way in which the conclusions of the decision analysis process will be ultimately presented. Thus, he may wish to obtain a description of something that takes place in his territory and of which he is not aware. Similarly, he may wish to obtain a hierarchization of all the decision objects. He may wish to obtain a selection of a subset of objects out of the general set of decision objects. Finally, he may want to have these objects classed into categories. These four issues, defined as "description", "ranking", "choice", and "sorting" or "scoring", respectively, may in practice arise in intertwined ways that an analyst will have to identify when the decision-maker's request is made or when the decision issues are described and structured.

10.4. Information, data, knowledge, uncertainties, and bias

The reader will have noticed that the models used in decision analysis rely on a constructivist approach. In this sense, the type of model chosen does not aim to limit the analyst's territory and decision to a deterministic model but to figure out the perceptions and preferences of the decision-makers, actors, and parties involved in what takes place in the territory affected by the decision, in order to make informed decisions in complex and disputed situations.

Thus, the information, data, and knowledge available to the analyst are of various kinds. They may involve maps, they may similarly derive from documentary sources, and they may also stem from surveys and interviews or even field investigations.

This information and these bodies of knowledge are affected by uncertainties about measurements, past or future temporal frameworks (what is probable and what is possible), knowledge, the ways of sharing and transferring lived experiences and perceptions and, finally, choices. The first two types of uncertainties are discussed in the previous chapters so we will not focus on their description and the ways of taking them into account here.

Let us consider the last two kinds of uncertainties. If uncertainty or risk is present, a set of psychological and cognitive mechanisms come into play when information is mobilized and related to the knowledge available. [KAH 82], [LIC 80], [SLO 80], [KAH 74], [SAN 93], and [RAC 99] have played a part in characterizing the factors that explain the differences in the perception of risks. The reader can find such a description in [MER 13]. [EPS 94] and [SLO 02] have also made a significant contribution to the distinction between the actors' ways of perceiving things in relation to the reasoning processes involved and they have managed to highlight two types of judgments, i.e. analytical and global.

The influence of culture and the sociocultural context ([DOU 82], [DOU 86] and [WAL 98]) on perception counterbalances the psycho-cognitive effect. This so-called cultural approach can highlight a certain number of contextual factors that vary depending on the territory. Finally, [REN 91] and [KAS 87] have illustrated how the effects of perceptions are accentuated in various circumstances.

A substantial part of the works on perception is descriptive. Research on judgment and perception bias is naturally descriptive, but it strives to provide a certain number of management strategies in decision sciences. Therefore, if each actor is affected by a certain number of factors that influence their perception of risks, it is necessary to identify strategies that aim to frame and prevent this type of perception bias. Four strategies can be identified in the literature (see especially [EPS 94], [FIS 82], [KAH 93], [SLO 02] and [STA 00]):

(i)   Warning about and reporting possible bias;

(ii)   Figuring out the consequences of this bias on the decision;

(iii) Sharing practical feedback;

(iv)   Creating and implementing coaching devices or even other measures taken to improve judgment.

It is important to note that there are countless promising strategies of this kind. Readers can refer to the literature listed above.

At the end of the phase that involves the description of the decision issues, the decision-analysis process can end. Let us point out that a decision-analysis process may be descriptive since, like prospective approaches, it helps to get rid of uncertainties about the awareness of the stakes of the decision and past and present conflicts as well as to reduce the risks involved in decision-making by decreasing the level of complexity perceived by the decision-maker.

This stage may similarly make it easier to redefine the boundaries of the framework, its features, and the territory of the decision and of the request.

This point needs highlighting. This redefinition of the boundaries of the decision issue does imply a certain number of conditions.

The first of these is the creation of a bond of trust between the decision-maker and the analyst which is not limited to the contract.

The second is related to the nature of the analyst's expertise. We have previously pointed out that a geographer is not a classic analyst. The latter simultaneously possesses methodological knowledge about the decision-support process and knowledge about territories and the various forms of spatialized knowledge. A geographer possesses, as it were, methodological knowledge as well as an "object" type of knowledge related to the decision. The decision-maker's acknowledgment of the specific features of the analyst's expertise, knowledge, and know-how plays a part in legitimizing the redefinition of the formal contractual framework.

Finally, the decision-maker needs to be aware of and acknowledge beforehand the effect of the modes of governance on the management of territorial issues that affect the general public. As these issues are rarely simple, since they concern and imply multiple actors (micro-, meso-, and macro-actors) and stakes, it is necessary to go beyond his perception of the decision issue which has been previously formalized in a contract.

10.5. Supporting the structuring and resolution of ranking, choice, or sorting problems (issues)

Let us consider the case in which a decision-maker or a sponsor chooses to request some decision analysis in the form of advice. At this point, an analyst faces a request for decision analysis that requires resort to a prescriptive approach.

At this point, with the approval of the decision-maker, it is the analyst who should reduce the initial descriptive complexity to a process where a decision issue is structured in light of a formal instantiation and the findings reported to the decision-maker. Figure 10.3 illustrates the key elements involved in structuring a decision issue. This structuring process amounts to describing the following set:

Pr- D = {DA, A, O, G, D, U, S, I}

which includes the pair Decision-Maker-Analyst (noted DA), the Actors (A), the Decision Objects (O), the modes of governance (G), the Data (D), the Uncertainties (U), the Stakes (S), as well as the Issues (I).

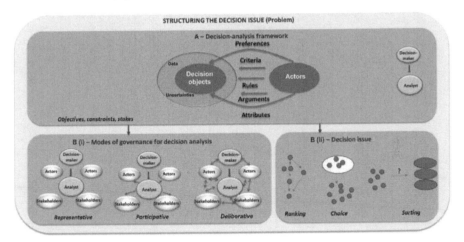

Figure 10.3. *The second phase in decision analysis: structuring the decision issue*

Choosing operational modes of governance for decision analysis creates a new context and a significant trend toward a stronger democracy with which the analyst must deal in addition to the decision-maker.

Participation, deliberation, and dialog are types of decision analysis that may take shape in various ways. They may be implemented thanks to an interface that has been formalized and instantiated beforehand by an analyst. This could involve a multi-actor GIS or another type of interactive interface. In this case, participation is said to be indirect, as there are no links between the analyst and the actors or between the decision-maker and the actors. Otherwise, we will refer to direct participation and deliberation operational modalities.

These differences are not trivial. In fact, they influence the choice of the formal rule that governs the decision and even the analysis of the decision.

Figure 10.4 describes the phase that concerns the analysis of the decision and summarizes the process that involves structuring the issue until the implementation of the conclusions.

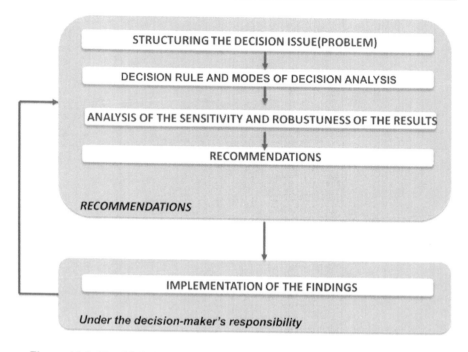

Figure 10.4. *The third phase: analyzing the decision and choosing a formal rule*

There are countless methods for analyzing a decision. Some of them are statistical (e.g. descriptive, principal component analysis, hierarchical classifications, etc.), while others involve multiple criteria, multiple agents, influence networks, and so on.

Practice tends to show that the choice of a rule or analytical method for a decision rarely constitutes an explicit and formal step. This choice is often the result of a community of practices, a scientific or cultural environment, or even a methodological similarity.

However, this choice could be made depending on the characteristics of the set Pr- D.

The following section aims to examine a type of method, i.e. multiple-criteria aggregation methods, in a specific context that concerns a request (asking for decision analysis) related to risk analysis and management.

10.6. A decision-analysis method for risk analysis and management

Like other methodological approaches, Multiple-Criteria Decision Analysis (MCDA) limits the observation of a decision-analysis situation to a certain number of integral elements:

– the actors (A) who will allow the analyst to identify a set of criteria and indicators as well as to figure out a more desirable and influential structure;

– some reference issues (Pr);

– some decision objects (O);

– a consistent family of criteria (CfC). A family of criteria is said to be consistent if it is exhaustive provided the problematic situation is analyzed, coherent (a criterion cannot provide conflicting information), and non-redundant (there must be no criteria that express the same thing). Some values are assigned to the criteria based on a scale that can reveal the performance of a decision object;

– an MCAP, which makes it possible to combine partial judgments about the decision objects, criterion by criterion, with a global (multiple-criteria) judgment about the decision object;

– Expression of robust conclusions about expertise or decision analysis.

Figure 10.5 summarizes these key steps.

Choosing an MCAP approach is not easy for an analyst. In this regard, we have previously suggested [MER 10] an approach where the aggregation procedure is chosen according to the level of uncertainty (U) and knowledge, the decision level and, therefore, the level of the stakes (S) involved, the issues in question (I), as well as the modes of governance (G) of decision analysis, and the type of interaction between the analyst and the decision-maker (DA).

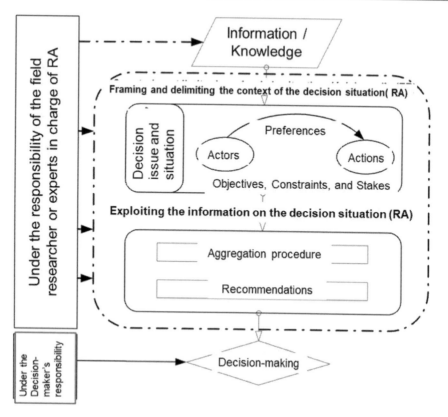

Figure 10.5. *An MCDA method used for risk analysis [MER 10]*

Figures 10.6 and 10.7 suggest an approach where an MCAP is chosen in relation to some decision-analysis issues in risk analysis and management.

Thus, the issue is to find the best approach out of various MCAPs: in a context where information and knowledge are heterogeneous and imprecise and involve a variety of actors, upgraded MCAPs have the advantage of structuring the field in which the actors interact. However, then they become hard to control and tricky to implement due to the number of parameters to establish. On the contrary, when information and knowledge tend to be more precise and the multiplicity of actors tends to be more reduced, then "unique synthetic criterion" MCAPs seem more suitable, even if they remain tricky due to their sensitivity to the values provided.

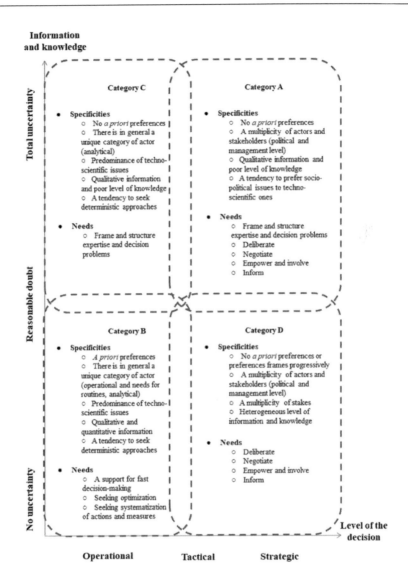

Figure 10.6. *Four types of risk analysis [MER 19]*

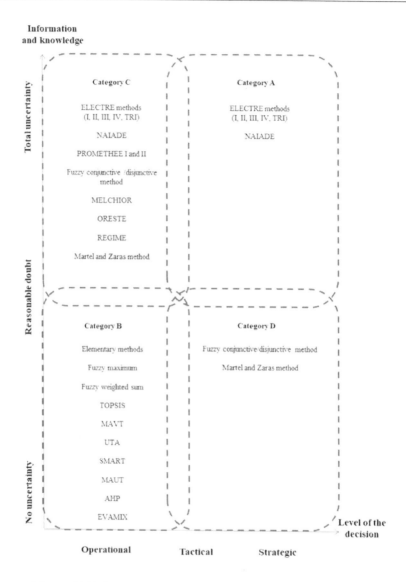

Figure 10.7. *A suggested MCAP by type of risk analysis [MER 19]*

10.7. Conclusion

The issues concerning uncertainty, risks, and complexity are the source of all the requests for decision analysis. This uncertainty affects data in a broad sense and takes shape in various ways which should not merely be quantified but also described properly and examined in relation to its effects on the structuring of the decision issue as well as the validity of the expertise conclusions.

Despite including a generic aspect, the decision-analysis process has some specific features when it is carried out by a geographer. In this chapter, we have attempted to summarize some specific characteristics and to redefine the relevant protocol.

We have also presented a type of decision-analysis approach, i.e. multiple-criteria approaches, and tried to shed light on a kind of issue (risk analysis) and on the choice of MCAPs. These procedures allow us, in a more or less suitable manner, to manage various types of uncertainties as well as different modes of governance. Each formalism underlying the aggregation methods is specific but also responds in a way to a common structure [MER 10].

A possible research perspective for these works could involve different decision analyses in geography in a risky and uncertain universe. Works on geo-governance like [BLE 13] and [DUB 15] will undoubtedly make a major contribution to the field.

10.8. References

[BLE 13] BLEY D., DUBUS N., MASSON-VINCENT M., *Géogouvernance: Utilité sociale de l'analyse spatiale*, Quae, Paris, 2013.

[DOU 82] DOUGLAS M., WILDAVSKY A., *Risk and Culture. An Essay on the Selection of Technological and Environmental Dangers*, University of California Press, Los Angeles, 1982.

[DOU 86] DOUGLAS M., *Risk Acceptability According to Social Sciences*, Routledge, London, 1986.

[DUB 15] DUBUS N., VOIRON-CANICIO C., EMSELLEM K. *et al.*, "Géogouvernance: l'espace comme médiateur et l'analyse spatiale comme vecteur de communication entre chercheurs et acteurs", *Chercheur.es et acteur.es de la participation: Liaisons dangereuses et relations fructueuses*, Saint-Denis, France, 29–30 January 2015.

[EPS 94] EPSTEIN S., "Integration of the cognitive and the psychodynamic unconscious", *American Psychologist*, vol. 49, pp. 709–724, 1994.

[KAH 74] KAHNEMAN D., TVERSKY A., "Judgment under uncertainty: heuristics and bias", *Science*, vol. 185, no. 4157, pp. 1124–1131, 1974.

[KAH 82] KAHNEMAN D., SLOVIC P., TVERSKY A., *Judgment Under Uncertainty: Huristics and Biases*, Cambridge University Press, Cambridge, 1982.

[KAH 93] KAHNEMAN D., LOVALLO D., "Timed choices and bold forecasts: a cognitive perspective on risk and risk taking", *Management Science*, no. 39, pp. 17–31, 1993.

[KAS 87] KASPERSON R., RENN O., SLOVIC P., "The social amplification of risk: a conceptual framework", *Risk Analysis*, vol. 8, pp. 177–187, 1987.

[MER 10] MERAD M., *Aide à la décision et expertise en gestion des risques*, Lavoisier, Paris, 2010.

[MER 13a] MERAD M., "Les compétences collectives au cœur des processus de gestion des risques: Histoire d'un processus de recherche-intervention au sein d'un Institut public d'expertise", in BREGEON J. (ed.), *Développement Durable : L'enjeu Compétences*, Editions ESKA, Paris, 2013.

[MER 13b] MERAD M., DECHY D., LLORY M. *et al.*, "Towards an analytics and an ethics of expertise: learning from decision aiding experiences in public risk assessment and risk management", *EURO Journal on Decision Processes*, vol. 2, nos 1–2, pp. 63–90, 2013.

[MER 19] MERAD M., TRUMP B., *Expertise Under Scrutiny: 21st Century Decision Making for Environmental Health and Safety*, Springer, Berlin, 2019.

[RAC 99] RECCHIA V., Risk communication and public perception of technological hazards, FEEM Working Paper No. 82.99, 1999.

[REN 91] RENN O., "Risk Communication and the Social Amplification of Risk", in KASPERSON R.E., STALLEN P.J.M. (eds), *Communicating Risks to the Public. Technology, Risk, and Society*, Kluwer Publishers, Amsterdam, 1991.

[SAN 93] SANDMAN P.M., *Responding to Community Outrage: Strategies for Effective Risk Communication*, American Industrial Hygiene Association, Fairfax, 1993.

[SLO 80] SLOVIC P., FISCHOFF B., LICHTENSTEIN S., *Facts and Fears: Understanding Perceived Risks. Society of Risk Assessments: How Safe is Safe Enough?*, Plenum Press, New York, 1980.

[SLO 02] SLOVIC P., FINUCANE M., PETERS E. *et al.*, "Rational actors or rational fools: implications of the affect heuristic for behavioral economics", *Journal of Socio-Economics*, vol. 31, pp. 329–342, 2002.

[STA 00] STANOVICH K.E., WEST R.F., "Individual differences in reasoning: implications for the rationality debate", *Behavioral and Brain Sciences*, vol. 23, pp. 645–726, 2000.

[WAL 98] WALKER G., SIMMS P., WYNNE B. *et al.*, Public perception of risks associated with major accidental hazards, Report, HSE, 1998.

List of Authors

Mireille BATTON-HUBERT
UMR 6158 LIMOS, CNRS
University of Clermont Auvergne
and
Institut Henri Fayol
École nationale supérieure des
mines de Saint-Étienne
France

Benjamin COSTÉ
Naval Cyber Defense
Brest
France

Nadine CULLOT
Laboratoire LIB
University of Burgundy
Dijon
France

Cyril DE RUNZ
CReSTIC
University of Reims
Champagne-Ardenne
France

Eric DESJARDIN
CReSTIC
University of Reims
Champagne-Ardenne
France

Rodolphe DEVILLERS
Department of Geography
Memorial University of
Newfoundland
St. John's
Canada

Jean-Michel FOLLIN
Laboratoire Géomatique et
Foncier (GEF)
École Supérieure des Géomètres
et Topographes
Conservatoire National des Arts
et Métiers
Le Mans
France

Giovanni FUSCO
ESPACE, CNRS
University of Côte d'Azur
Nice
France

Élisabeth GAVIGNET
Laboratoire LIB
University of Burgundy
Dijon
France

Jean-François GIRRES
UMR GRED
Paul Valéry University
Montpellier III – IRD
France

Clément IPHAR
Centre for Maritime Research and
Experimentation
NATO Science & Technology
Organization
and
Centre for Research on Risks and
Crises (CRC)
MINES ParisTech
PSL Research University
Sophia Antipolis
France

Florence LE BER
ICube Laboratory
CNRS, ENGEES
University of Strasbourg
France

Myriam MERAD
ESPACE, CNRS
University of Côte d'Azur
Nice
and
LAMSADE, CNRS
Paris-Dauphine University PSL
France

Aldo NAPOLI
Centre for Research on Risks and
Crises (CRC)
MINES ParisTech
PSL Research University
Sophia Antipolis
France

Ana-Maria OLTEANU-RAIMOND
LaSTIG-COGIT – IGN
École Nationale des Sciences
Géographiques
Saint-Mandé
France

François PINET
Irstea, TSCF research unit
Clermont-Ferrand
France

Cyril RAY
IRENav
Ecole navale
Lanvéoc
France

David SHEEREN
UMR DYNAFOR
École Nationale Supérieure
Agronomique de Toulouse
National Polytechnic Institute of
Toulouse
France

Andrea TETTAMANZI
I3S, INRIA, CNRS
University of Côte d'Azur
Nice
France

Index

2018

ARDUIN Pierre-Emmanuel
Insider Threats
(Advances in Information Systems Set – Volume 10)

CARMÈS Maryse
Digital Organizations Manufacturing: Scripts, Performativity and Semiopolitics
(Intellectual Technologies Set – Volume 5)

CARRÉ Dominique, VIDAL Geneviève
Hyperconnectivity: Economical, Social and Environmental Challenges
(Computing and Connected Society Set – Volume 3)

CHAMOUX Jean-Pierre
The Digital Era 1: Big Data Stakes

DOUAY Nicolas
Urban Planning in the Digital Age
(Intellectual Technologies Set – Volume 6)

FABRE Renaud, BENSOUSSAN Alain
The Digital Factory for Knowledge: Production and Validation of Scientific Results

GAUDIN Thierry, LACROIX Dominique, MAUREL Marie-Christine, POMEROL Jean-Charles
Life Sciences, Information Sciences

GAYARD Laurent
Darknet: Geopolitics and Uses
(Computing and Connected Society Set – Volume 2)

IAFRATE Fernando
Artificial Intelligence and Big Data: The Birth of a New Intelligence
(Advances in Information Systems Set – Volume 8)

LE DEUFF Olivier
Digital Humanities: History and Development
(Intellectual Technologies Set – Volume 4)

MANDRAN Nadine
Traceable Human Experiment Design Research: Theoretical Model and Practical Guide
(Advances in Information Systems Set – Volume 9)

PIVERT Olivier
NoSQL Data Models: Trends and Challenges

ROCHET Claude
Smart Cities: Reality or Fiction

SAUVAGNARGUES Sophie
Decision-making in Crisis Situations: Research and Innovation for Optimal Training

SEDKAOUI Soraya
Data Analytics and Big Data

SZONIECKY Samuel
Ecosystems Knowledge: Modeling and Analysis Method for Information and Communication
(Digital Tools and Uses Set – Volume 6)

2017

BOUHAÏ Nasreddine, SALEH Imad
Internet of Things: Evolutions and Innovations
(Digital Tools and Uses Set – Volume 4)

DUONG Véronique
Baidu SEO: Challenges and Intricacies of Marketing in China

LESAS Anne-Marie, MIRANDA Serge
The Art and Science of NFC Programming
(Intellectual Technologies Set – Volume 3)

LIEM André
Prospective Ergonomics
(Human-Machine Interaction Set – Volume 4)

MARSAULT Xavier
Eco-generative Design for Early Stages of Architecture
(Architecture and Computer Science Set – Volume 1)

REYES-GARCIA Everardo
The Image-Interface: Graphical Supports for Visual Information
(Digital Tools and Uses Set – Volume 3)

REYES-GARCIA Everardo, BOUHAÏ Nasreddine
Designing Interactive Hypermedia Systems
(Digital Tools and Uses Set – Volume 2)

SAÏD Karim, BAHRI KORBI Fadia
Asymmetric Alliances and Information Systems:Issues and Prospects
(Advances in Information Systems Set – Volume 7)

SZONIECKY Samuel, BOUHAÏ Nasreddine
*Collective Intelligence and Digital Archives: Towards Knowledge
Ecosystems*
(Digital Tools and Uses Set – Volume 1)

2016

BEN CHOUIKHA Mona
Organizational Design for Knowledge Management

BERTOLO David
Interactions on Digital Tablets in the Context of 3D Geometry Learning
(Human-Machine Interaction Set – Volume 2)

BOUVARD Patricia, SUZANNE Hervé
Collective Intelligence Development in Business

EL FALLAH SEGHROUCHNI Amal, ISHIKAWA Fuyuki, HÉRAULT Laurent,
TOKUDA Hideyuki
Enablers for Smart Cities

FABRE Renaud, in collaboration with MESSERSCHMIDT-MARIET Quentin,
HOLVOET Margot
New Challenges for Knowledge

VENTRE Daniel
Chinese Cybersecurity and Defense

2013

BERNIK Igor
Cybercrime and Cyberwarfare

CAPET Philippe, DELAVALLADE Thomas
Information Evaluation

LEBRATY Jean-Fabrice, LOBRE-LEBRATY Katia
Crowdsourcing: One Step Beyond

SALLABERRY Christian
Geographical Information Retrieval in Textual Corpora

2012

BUCHER Bénédicte, LE BER Florence
Innovative Software Development in GIS

GAUSSIER Eric, YVON François
Textual Information Access

STOCKINGER Peter
Audiovisual Archives: Digital Text and Discourse Analysis

VENTRE Daniel
Cyber Conflict

2011

BANOS Arnaud, THÉVENIN Thomas
Geographical Information and Urban Transport Systems

DAUPHINÉ André
Fractal Geography

LEMBERGER Pirmin, MOREL Mederic
Managing Complexity of Information Systems

STOCKINGER Peter
Introduction to Audiovisual Archives

STOCKINGER Peter
Digital Audiovisual Archives

VENTRE Daniel
Cyberwar and Information Warfare

2010

BONNET Pierre
Enterprise Data Governance

BRUNET Roger
Sustainable Geography

CARREGA Pierre
Geographical Information and Climatology

CAUVIN Colette, ESCOBAR Francisco, SERRADJ Aziz
Thematic Cartography – 3-volume series
Thematic Cartography and Transformations – Volume 1
Cartography and the Impact of the Quantitative Revolution – Volume 2
New Approaches in Thematic Cartography – Volume 3

LANGLOIS Patrice
Simulation of Complex Systems in GIS

MATHIS Philippe
Graphs and Networks – 2nd edition

THERIAULT Marius, DES ROSIERS François
Modeling Urban Dynamics

2009

BONNET Pierre, DETAVERNIER Jean-Michel, VAUQUIER Dominique
Sustainable IT Architecture: the Progressive Way of Overhauling
Information Systems with SOA

PAPY Fabrice
Information Science

RIVARD François, ABOU HARB Georges, MERET Philippe
The Transverse Information System

ROCHE Stéphane, CARON Claude
Organizational Facets of GIS

2008

BRUGNOT Gérard
Spatial Management of Risks

FINKE Gerd
Operations Research and Networks

GUERMOND Yves
Modeling Process in Geography

KANEVSKI Michael
Advanced Mapping of Environmental Data

MANOUVRIER Bernard, LAURENT Ménard
Application Integration: EAI, B2B, BPM and SOA

PAPY Fabrice
Digital Libraries

2007

DOBESCH Hartwig, DUMOLARD Pierre, DYRAS Izabela
Spatial Interpolation for Climate Data

SANDERS Lena
Models in Spatial Analysis

2006

CLIQUET Gérard
Geomarketing

CORNIOU Jean-Pierre
Looking Back and Going Forward in IT

DEVILLERS Rodolphe, JEANSOULIN Robert
Fundamentals of Spatial Data Quality

Printed and bound by CPI Group (UK) Ltd, Croydon, CR0 4YY